"One of the hardest things to see about my generation is complete fear of pain or dealing w[...] wounds, hoping they'll go away, b[...] that brokenness is actually the very [...] and the place where we can find Je[...] wait to see this book unleashed to t[...]

Jefferson Bethke, *New York Times* bestselling author of *Jesus > Religion*

"Mo Isom's book, *Wreck My Life: Journeying from Broken to Bold*, is a raw and honest story of her trek from a cracked and hopeless life to one of healing and restoration found only in Jesus. Mo can truly say now that her self-worth comes from her complete dependence on Christ. Joy comes to her and to all of us by saying yes to Jesus. This book will bring you hope in your own journey, and you'll find yourself celebrating not just her life but your own."

Shelley Giglio, cofounder of Passion Conferences/Passion City Church; chief strategist of sixstepsrecords

"I first read part of Mo's story in an online article and was so moved by her transparency and how she persevered through all she has been through. In *Wreck My Life*, Mo tells the amazing story of God's grace and redemption in her life as He uses what was broken and makes it beautiful. It's a reminder that we serve a God who never fails to meet us where we are and promises to give us beauty for ashes. You will find life and grace as you turn each page."

Melanie Shankle, *New York Times* bestselling author of *Nobody's Cuter Than You*

"Mo Isom is an incredible communicator, both from the stage and in her writing. It takes a lot of heart to combine your own personal and heartbreaking stories with life lessons and biblical truths and do so with humor, candor, and honesty, but Mo has done it. Every person who picks up this book will be challenged, entertained, and more connected with God by reading it."

Annie Downs, author of *Let's All Be Brave*

"In a generation that lacks authenticity, *Wreck My Life* shines bright. Mo's raw, real, and unfiltered story will captivate you in a way others can't. *Everyone* can relate to the real-life issues tackled in this book, and everyone *needs* the hope it provides."

Sam Acho, NFL linebacker; humanitarian

"First of all, if I had a little sister, I'd want her to be just like Mo Isom: fearless, compassionate, hardworking, and *deeply* funny. Second of all, when I sat down with my copy of *Wreck My Life*, my plan was to read one chapter. Just one. Two hours later, however, I looked up and realized that I'd been completely engrossed in Mo's story—a story that's heartbreaking, relatable, inspiring, and redemptive. Mo's words are such a reminder that we serve a good God who faithfully rescues us from the wreckage of our lives, a God whose plans for us are so much more than we could ask or imagine (Eph. 3:20). By the end of this book, you'll feel like Mo is a longtime friend and you'll be better for the time you've spent with her. (Also: you *may* start to think about trying out for a spot on the LSU football team, but just know that will fade with time. It did for me. But it's possible that I may have tried to punt my son's football. I blame Mo.) Don't miss this phenomenal book!"

Sophie Hudson, author of *Giddy Up, Eunice*
and *Home Is Where My People Are*

"It's said that 'the struggle is real.' In *Wreck My Life*, Mo Isom is a tour guide who leads you to the center of some very real struggles. But she doesn't leave you there. She crafts a life-giving narrative chock-full of Scripture and stories that will help connect the personal details of your greatest challenges with the pervasive hope, healing, and freedom found in Jesus Christ."

Gwen Smith, speaker; worship leader;
cofounder of Girlfriends in God;
author of *Broken into Beautiful*
and *I Want It ALL*

"No one wants pain. No one seeks out brokenness. But Mo Isom reminds us that when those things come our way, they are exactly what God uses to form us into people He can use."

Danny Wuerffel, 1996 Heisman Trophy winner;
executive director of Desire Street Ministries

# WRECK
## my life

Journeying from Broken to Bold

# MO ISOM

**BakerBooks**
*a division of Baker Publishing Group*
Grand Rapids, Michigan

© 2016 by Mo Isom

Published by Baker Books
a division of Baker Publishing Group
P.O. Box 6287, Grand Rapids, MI 49516-6287
www.bakerbooks.com

Printed in the United States of America

Library of Congress Cataloging-in-Publication Data
Names: Isom, Mo, 1989– author.
Title: Wreck my life : journeying from broken to bold / Mo Isom.
Description: Grand Rapids : Baker Books, 2016.
Identifiers: LCCN 2016001362 | ISBN 9780801008146 (pbk.)
Subjects: LCSH: Consolation. | Suffering—Religious aspects—Christianity. | Isom, Mo, 1989–
Classification: LCC BV4905.3 .I86 2016 | DDC 248.8/6—dc23
LC record available at https://lccn.loc.gov/2016001362

Some names and details have been changed to protect the privacy of the individuals involved.

16   17   18   19   20   21   22      7   6   5   4   3   2   1

In keeping with biblical principles of creation stewardship, Baker Publishing Group advocates the responsible use of our natural resources. As a member of the Green Press Initiative, our company uses recycled paper when possible. The text paper of this book is composed in part of post-consumer waste.

For Big John

# Contents

# Introduction

I have told you these things, so that in me you may have
peace. In this world you *will* have trouble. But take heart!
I have overcome the world.

John 16:33, emphasis added

Scripture makes many promises.

This particular verse is one that was always difficult for me.
It was hard to *really* believe. Who wants to wholeheartedly
embrace a guarantee of life-altering pain and unexpected tri-
als? A promise that if you haven't already been in a storm, or
if you aren't standing in one right now, then there is certainly
one on the horizon. A promise of *wreckage*, in some shape or
form. Wreckage that could stand to disrupt everything. It's
scary, right? To think that no matter how hard we hope we
can move through this life unscathed, we're bound for trouble
somewhere along the way.

I didn't want to hear it.

Somewhere along the way I bought into the lie that a blessed life was a life lived with as little hardship as possible. That I was entitled to comfort and ease and happiness. That God was most present and pleased in the lives of those with abundance and minimal adversity. Rather than wrapping my head around the truth that hardship was inevitable, I convinced myself that if I did the right things and said the right things then maybe I could play it safe enough. So I flipped through the pages of life-breathed Scripture looking for the nearest inspirational verse instead of digging into the ones that made me ache and confused me. A quick pick-me-up. As if I could pick and choose what I wanted to be applicable to my own story. I moved through my days under the impression that *I* was the author of my story and that the trajectory of my life solely depended on my control, my success, and my own personal strength.

Because of my skewed perception of reality, when the promised hardship did come my way it came close to ending me. When trouble came I desperately clung to my ability to cope with and mask and hold together all of the broken pieces. I lost myself trying to save myself and compromised so many things. I strove to be whole again—as if my own broken hands could ever fix my mangled heart. As if my ability to save my own story would somehow warrant me more personal glory when the world took its best look at me. And, in turn, I ended up wasting many of my younger years. Not listening. Not learning.

I don't want that for you.

Suffering, adversity, and discomfort often derail us and drag us into a downward spiral of depression, blame, and pity. We wander through our days drowned in social media, social pressure, and spiritual timidity. In a culture of "fake it till you make it," we keep our struggles to ourselves and only put our best foot forward for the world to reward. As a result, we're becoming broken, lonely people who feel isolated in our sin struggles and ashamed of our shattered pieces. In a culture that craves comfort, we blame God for our wreckage, we doubt His goodness and sovereignty, and oftentimes we turn our back on a God we don't believe could be truly loving and good if He allows such pain and suffering.

I didn't want to hear it either, but what if in our haste to feel good and avoid discomfort we're ignoring promises that aren't meant to *scare* us but rather *prepare* us? What if we're missing out on the resounding glory of a sovereign King who is stating the obvious? He knows His opponent. He knows life is challenging and invites us to armor up on His team. This King gently promises us that we will all walk through valleys but in Him we are offered a divine hope in the depths of defeat.

What if hearing and accepting the hardest things is exactly what sets us free? What if we began to recognize trouble and adversity as sacred rather than scarring? As promised rather than unforeseen? As guaranteed rather than game-changing? As purposeful rather than punishing? What if we truly believed there was purpose in our pain and a plan in our persecution? What would our world look like if we shifted our mentality and began to rejoice in our adversity, knowing adversity produces perseverance, perseverance produces character, and character produces hope (see Rom. 5:3–5)?

What if we began to lean in to the second portion of John 16:33 that clearly promises there is something more—*someone more*—who has already triumphed over our defeat? A promise that introduces Jesus and wrecks through religion and begins to mean something. A promise of victory that looks like an innocent Judge taking on a death sentence so we, the criminals, can be set free. A promise that looks like a King who wrote the story of the cross, and all that it means, into the fingerprints of our genealogy. A promise that suddenly invites the holy words of Scripture to crawl off of the page, to breathe into our life—to wreck and redefine everything.

In a broken world, our adversity and suffering will not cease but our perspective can boldly shift. We can begin to embrace adversity in a new light. We can begin to surrender the pain and suffering of our past, accept the forgiveness and grace offered in the present, and invite a holy God to *wreck our lives*. To unhinge the lies we've believed, to shake our preconceived ideas and beliefs, to obliterate our bondage and our shame and our pride and our defeat. With radical, unshakable faith placed in a radical, unfailing King, we are able to appreciate the wreckage of our past and orchestrate the voluntary wreckage of our future for the glory of a King who was first wrecked on our behalf.

I want to share my story with you in hopes that it becomes your story too. I hope this testimony serves as a framework, one you can read through and transfuse your own story into. I hope these words find the pilgrim whose gasping breath cries out for life-saving truth and authenticity and peace. I hope these words find the nonbeliever in silent search of something more. I hope these words meet the scorned believer creeping back to a place of trust and that they also speak to the faithful believer, empowered and encouraged by the word of testimony.

This book is full of things that challenge me and make me ache—the things that I always find hard to believe—particularly when my soul and flesh yearn for very different things. At its core, it's about a messy *King* story that intervenes with a messy *me* story and somehow comes together for *His glory* in spite of everything. The heart of this testimony stares involuntary wreckage in the eyes and declares, "This will not win my story." It invites voluntary wreckage and kneels before a King and says, "I am Yours and You are mine. Will you humble my wandering heart and wreck me for Your glory?"

I hope this book invites you to crawl out of your grief and step into the excitement of how God plans to use you; not seeing your new journey as a reluctant Plan B but as the Master Plan tailored to your perfectly imperfect life. You may be feeling empty as you pick up this book. I pray it connects with you and helps you make some sense of the broken things. That it holds your hand and invites you to sit in the midst of a far greater story. That it encourages you to believe.

So let's strip away the formality. Right now it's just you and me. In this world, we *will* face trouble. And usually, that's the start of our story.

# 1

## The Breaking Point

I was as wounded and scabbed and scarred as they come. All I wanted to do was forget. But I couldn't just forget. I couldn't forget the image of his body on a morgue table. I couldn't forget the feeling that his love for me hadn't been strong enough to change the outcome of that day.

And I couldn't sit still long enough to let my wounds heal because all I wanted to do was run.

Thanksgiving break couldn't come soon enough. I needed out. Out of the college town that sung my praises, even when my depression drowned out their cheers. I needed home. The arms of my mom and the safety of a place where I could take off my mask and stop acting like I was strong. I needed rest. I was tired and empty and so sick of faking "fine."

My last day before break had been filled with distraction after distraction, task after task that popped up and *had* to be finished before I could head home to Georgia—an eight-hour drive from Louisiana's capitol. A drive I had made so many times before. But something about this time was different. The year had taken more of a toll on me than I even realized. I was anxious and restless and found it hard to shake the resentment that tightened my tired muscles. I was eager to leave the day and to abandon the moment, to drive in hopes that I would forget all the moments that came before it. Even just for a little while.

By the time I finally finished everything I had to do and hit the road, it was nearing five p.m. When I pulled onto the interstate, it quickly became apparent I wasn't the only one eager to head home for the holidays. In fact, the entire population of Baton Rouge seemed to be parked on the freeway. After about two hours I had only moved about two miles. When the traffic finally broke, my eight-hour drive had become a ten-hour drive and I had the road rage to prove it.

But I drove. And drove. And drove.

For a while I let my mind be hypnotized by the passing street lines. *Zip. Zip. Zip. Zip.* They flew past like fireflies as dusk settled and my restless day turned into my anxious night. A part of me felt reckless—never fully present in a moment or concerned with anything more than the pain of my past and the hopelessness of the "now." My whole year had felt that way.

I texted a few guys on my phone as I sat, stuck, dragging through stop-and-go traffic. One in particular was bad for me. Or should I say, I was bad for him. I was bad for all of them. But that had never stopped me from getting my fix before. The year had left a gaping hole in my heart, and the brokenness that riddled my bones was only ever temporarily fixed by the encouraging words of friends and family. My loss hadn't just left me broken, it had left me desperate. And desperate girls do desperate things when they don't feel loved.

This guy was no different from every other one before him, and my intentions were no more pure than they had been with those others. It felt good to know that I could make a man desire me with just a few words. It felt good to know I'd have a hookup waiting at home. As I gave myself away to the imagination of a man who wouldn't matter, a part of me felt powerful again. A part of me felt like I was in control.

Another part of me knew it was wrong. It was all wrong. It had all been wrong for the longest time. I wasn't ignorant of the spiritual warfare that was ripping me at the seams, I was just too numb to fight it anymore. The tension was unceasing—it had been for a while. And rather than fight to seek hope and find a solution, I just absorbed it. I absorbed that tension into the DNA of my character and came to a halfhearted peace that things were as good as they were going to get. This unsettled angst was my new norm, and if I wanted to feel okay I just needed to accept that and move forward.

It's hard to describe what the tension of warfare feels like. For me it was a constant tugging in my chest, a tightness that was only eased by sitting through a church service and hoping that counted for something—or by drinking myself numb or distracting myself with men or drowning myself in my work and my athletics. So I did all of these things well—anything to pretend everything was all right. Anything to be affirmed and to feel wanted. But the tension hadn't ceased through the year. If anything, it had only grown stronger and tighter, clenching me like the grip of a father who refused to let go of a thrashing child.

Like the grip of *the Father* who refused to let go of my wandering soul.

I was apathetic on the outside but screaming on the inside. Screaming that this wasn't the life I had planned. Screaming to a God whom I proclaimed to love but in the depths of my heart doubted was even good. Screaming in frustration that I even cared so much! How weak I must be—what a pathetic, soft woman, that my emotions and my pain could rule my days.

I felt captive to the world's perception of me. A slave to pretending that I was healing, giving prepackaged glory to a God I didn't know. My lips stayed sealed with my practiced smile but my mind was shouting for freedom. I was at the breaking point, ravaged by my internal battle. It had been a year of anguish, preceded by several years of feeling lost, then found, then lost again. It seemed like I was on a roller-coaster ride and my heart wanted off. I was done!

My car continued to speed down the interstate as night crept into morning. Even though the mile markers assured me I was headed home, I felt like I was crawling. The hours dragged by and my eyes hung heavy and my phone kept buzzing and all of it was just annoying.

Then it was one in the morning and I realized that, for the most part, I was the only car on the road. I spotted a few glowing deer eyes in the woods as I passed, but they were hard to catch amid the fog. The fog began to thicken, until it was so dense it blanketed the street and swirled up from the median. My car split through it at eighty miles per hour as I slumped, mentally numb, in the driver's seat.

It would almost be easier not to care. Easier to crawl between the sheets of a "friend" and keep secrets of what happened in the dark, to talk the talk and rest in the lies and accept the praise. After all, I knew all the right things to say—whether they were truthful or not. I could just take the depression meds and convince myself they'd work one day. I could just laugh along with the world's sense of humor and be entertained by the newest craze. It would be easier to fall back into my pity when the tension was too tight. To blame my behavior on the scars of my circumstances and to rationalize that it would someday all be fine.

It would almost be easier to exalt my wreckage than to seek the seemingly fleeting God who had wrecked Himself on my behalf. If the year had convinced me of anything, it was that *this* God, the God everyone shoved down my throat, the Healer and Redeemer and Restorer, was far, far away from me. Sure, I was good at regurgitating memorized praises, but in my broken, burned-out state, my calloused heart prayed not for salvation or for strength but for proof. For months I'd pleaded for proof.

*Prove it. If You're so real, if You love me the way everyone says You do, reveal Yourself to me. I want what everyone else seems to have and if somehow that's from You, give it to me! Prove it!*

In desperation I'd spent months petitioning a God whom I demanded cater to my need for proof. I'd tried fighting the tension by demanding God fix my circumstances and bless me out of my mess. I half-believed He might—and half-believed my prayers were a last-ditch effort I could pretend I hadn't been desperate enough to pray, if anyone asked, when still nothing had changed.

I'd tried challenging God into restoring my brokenness, never realizing that He heard my cries and knew my brokenness better than I knew myself. Never realizing that my pleas for revelation were about to be answered by a Father who wasn't trying to preserve me but rather was willing to wreck me for His glory.

A Father who'd been waiting for such a time as this—to wreck my life.

I glanced over to see a sign glowing green in the night. *Atlanta—100 miles.* Thank goodness. I was nearing the state line and home was almost in sight.

When I caught the road again, the fog was dense and spinning. Before I could make sense of the moment, my steering wheel began to jolt and jerk. Cranking side to side, I realized my wheels were twisting through mud and grass. I had been speeding down the left lane and was now dropping off the side of the road. My mind snapped out of its haze and, in desperation, I clenched the cold leather wheel and pulled it hard to the right.

*Get back on the road! Get back on the road!*

My heart pounded and my muscles tensed in fear as I tried desperately to regain control. The fog split and I saw the front of my Jeep speeding forward almost completely perpendicular to the lines on the asphalt.

*No! No! This can't happen! Get back on the road!*

My Jeep lunged back onto the pavement and charged straight over it toward a wooded embankment. I desperately pulled back to the left as my wheel caught a deep divot—and in the deepest parts of me I knew it was over.

My body gave way to the force that was overwhelming my car. Fear paralyzed me. A piercing, screaming, indescribable type of fear. A fear that flooded me as fast as a rushing waterfall but forced time to slow to a drip. My stomach felt as though it might bulge up into my throat as I realized my equilibrium was way off. I closed my eyes, took a deep breath in, and let out a gut-wrenching groan as metal screeched and glass shattered.

My body slapped and ripped against itself, the window, the side of the car, the steering wheel. My ears rung as the sounds of destruction roared and my neck whipped with the rolling, wrenching force.

My eyes tore open in time to see a steel signpost speeding closer. Then muddy ground. The empty street. The freezing, dark sky.

My head burned and my eyes stung and debris pounded against my face. The noise only grew louder and I realized, as I choked back some unknown heat, that half of that noise was roaring out of me. My body thrashed and whipped and coiled and—

*Slam!*

Everything went black.

# 2

# Buying into Wrecked Religion

When I was growing up, my family looked good on the outside. Really good. We all begin with the best of intentions. Wreckage is never planned.

As a young child I was oblivious to the tension that was slowly growing tighter behind closed doors. You could have convinced me my parents were superheroes and our house was a palace. I was unaware of how much the cracks in the foundations of our family would affect me later on. It's beautiful, really—the mind of a child. Content with the simplest treasures and captivated by the tiniest joys.

My family lived in a middle-class Georgia suburb that often liked to act like it was a little wealthier than its bank accounts might have proven. But my house nestled itself deep in a warm neighborhood that always seemed to welcome us, and the walls of our Cape Cod–style home creaked with decades of laughter and tears and frustrations and *life*. We weren't the wealthiest family, but we lived well.

I was a stubborn, bullheaded child with a big imagination and even bigger brown eyes. What I lacked in grace I made up for in grit. My mom and dad learned quickly that it was going to take a unique style of parenting to bend my unbridled will without breaking it. I'd like to argue those features have come full circle to serve me well in life, but the massive bald spot on my dad's head and the gray my mom still dyes out of her hair might sing a different tune.

My parents seemed to be all that a young girl's parents should be—supportive, passionate, encouraging, patient, strict, loving, and proud. If you stared long enough into my mom's gentle eyes, you could see the same flames of passion and drive that licked in the twinkle of my own. She was fabulous. And theatrical. And larger than life to a young girl who was hungry for life in its fullest.

I may have titled myself a "daddy's girl" and chosen to sweat far more often than I smiled, but there was something about my mom that mesmerized me. When I wasn't building forts barefoot in the woods, I was using the shaving cream cap to scrape imaginary hair off my legs and copying a mommy who made beauty seem effortless. When I wasn't rolling around on muddy soccer fields, I was rolling on the floor of her home office, admiring how fast she typed and how confidently she took calls.

Her scent was intoxicating, as was her courage. I think that's why the few times I stumbled in on her crying, I never quite knew how to act. And when the man standing across from her with an embarrassed look quickly turned the conversation, all I knew to do was laugh in his arms and believe everything would be fine. After all, he was my hero. I was my daddy's girl.

His size alone commanded a room—but his deeply bronzed skin served well to soften his imposing frame. He was quick to crack jokes and even quicker to crack a sly smile, with his crooked front teeth and his infectious ease. I was convinced my dad was invincible—the picture of strength and love. If he wasn't waking me up, bounding up onto my bed with all three hundred pounds of his belly, he was playing oldies through the house and firing up the grill. He may have been an attorney by trade, but he was just an Alabama boy at heart. He was so easy for a child to love because oftentimes he believed he was still a child too.

My older sister, Sloan, and I were my parents' greatest prizes, but I'd like to think the tomboy in me fed my dad's particular hope for an athlete in the family. His college football days at Carson Newman were long since passed, though he had plenty of scars that told tales of first downs and Saturday night glory. As for Sloan, sports were not quite her thing. Piano keys replaced cleat laces and her love for science transformed one of our home closets into a miniature laboratory.

She and I could not have been more different. I was a wrecking ball with loud, stubborn confidence and she was the truest of introverts who wisped about in silence and with charm. She was a firstborn in every sense, fully content with her nose in a good book and the spotlight directed far away from her. If the people around her were pleased and appeased, then she was happy. And the fact that she survived being *my* big sister says a lot more about her strength and wit than I could ever write.

I loved my family. Fiercely. As a child, I loved the life we were blessed to live. We had all the ingredients and all the pieces in place, it seemed. But in many ways, that was a dangerous thing.

25

I think it's a bit of a catch-22 to grow up living a privileged, comfortable life. The parents know how much work it takes to keep everything balanced and how much sacrifice it takes to provide a pleasurable life for their kids, but in the children's eyes—in mine, at least—it all just ends up looking easy.

We don't know trouble because we're protected from it. We don't know hardship because those who love us take the blows for us. Somewhere along the line we begin to assume we're entitled to this protection, that it's a given. We begin to realize that if we want to continue receiving this love and praise it's wise to go with the flow. We memorize how to follow in the footsteps of our family. A trait that, in many ways, can benefit our earthly lives, but if we're not careful can risk our eternal ones.

## A Faith by Inheritance

I followed my family's footsteps right into wrecked religion. I wonder how many of us have done the same. That's not to say Christianity itself was broken or flawed, or that our church was doing a sub-par job. In fact, our church was incredible, and led well by those living boldly in God's will. But *my* perspective of the faith was far off-base, and it seemed that no amount of preaching could compel that to change.

My mom worked hard to instill in my sister and me what it meant to be godly women. She shared her faith. She answered our questions. She clung to the cross. But in my eyes it was just a part of our family's weekly routine. To be honest, church on Sunday felt as mundane as school on a weekday. As expected as soccer practice on a Tuesday. As dreaded as homework at night. It was just another one of those "things" we had to do.

I guess I assumed that showing up made me a Christian. That somehow my attendance qualified me. I mean, my parents were Christians. That alone was enough of a defining factor, right? I had grown up hearing all about Jesus, God, and the cross. I must have heard the gospel ten thousand times. Surely that counted for something. I knew all *about* God. I knew that Jesus died for my sins. I guess what I missed was why it was supposed to matter.

The truth was, in my mind, being a Christian was expected. Religion was just another piece to the puzzle of a well-lived life.

If you had asked me then, I would have said there were certain things that made someone a Christian. Things we were supposed to do. I was supposed to dress up on Sundays and go to church. I was supposed to listen to the teachings and sing the hymns and read my Bible. On our drive home, I was supposed to talk about what the pastor had taught us. I was supposed to pray. I was supposed to do good things—to do the right things. I was supposed to be a good person.

I didn't ask too many questions beyond that. The stories were compelling and the teachings were encouraging and sometimes I'd walk away having felt something special. But, in truth, I didn't even really care enough about religion to think any further about it than the two hours on Sunday where I was required to find God relevant.

I was comfortable with God in a box and church on a checklist and a cross on my necklace. As if my seat in a pew reserved me a seat in heaven.

What's scary is that this mentality is ultimately where my brokenness began and, at the same time, what seemed normal and comfortable. My simpleminded perspective of faith was that Christianity was more an expectation than a radical revelation. Religion was a way to guide people's behaviors—an encouraging outlet for inspiration.

It's no wonder church was a "to-do" on my checklist. I knew all about God but didn't truly know God, and I had no idea there was a difference. I was comfortable enough with showing my face in church and hoping one day, when I stood before the Lord, some of my friends and family would stand beside me and remind God just how many times I had shown up and what a good person I was.

What I didn't realize at the time was that showing our face doesn't earn us grace. When we stand before the Lord, we will stand alone. We're selling ourselves short when we shrink the house of the Lord to the size of a ticket that hopefully we can punch when we die. Going through the motions can only entertain us for so long. Eventually, the gospel will feel canned when it's preached to us. When it's preached *at* us. We'll sit unfazed and dying as lifesaving news goes in one ear and out the other. Like skeletons lining the church pews hoping that if we attend enough at some point we'll come back to life. But our hearts know better and will yearn for something more. And in our hope that the world will give more to us, we'll put broken things on a pedestal and rely on them to teach us what we haven't seemed to learn. We'll put God-sized expectations on the people around us. When imperfect people fall short and fail us, we'll build a false perception of an imperfect God who will inevitably do the same.

## Exalting Wrecked Idols

We all have that person who paints our picture of love. The person we exalt as somehow more than human. The one we

28

always trust will have open arms when we come running. The one we turn to with our questions and concerns.

They're the person whose love for us defines, in our minds, what love must really mean. We hold on to them tightly. We lift them up as mighty. When we hear talk about a God who *is* love, we believe this person must be the closest thing.

But the closest thing is never actually *the* thing. And when we try to fit a human being into a God-sized mold, we're bound for disappointment somewhere along the way. Because people are not perfect. People will fail us. When a conditional person frames our understanding of unconditional love, our hearts can be left confused. When that person falls short, we'll believe love has fallen short. And when that person fails us, we'll think love has failed us. We'll all end up in the same place—walking on eggshells to maintain a fragile love that requires more than any person can give.

That person for me was my daddy. Oh, how I loved him. He was my very best friend. I remember that when I was little I would woefully explain to my mom that she should enjoy her years with Daddy. Because when I got big enough and grew up he was going to be my husband too.

No man could compare to the daddy who wrapped me up in big bear hugs and who threw me up on his shoulders when my legs were tired. The man who sat through my pajama-clad Spice Girls performances and tickled my knee every time I rode shotgun in his old silver truck. The man who drove me to every soccer practice, every game, and every camp. Who toted me along to Braves games and cheered beside me when we made it onto the Jumbotron. The one who fought for me, provided for me, and believed in me.

No man could come close to *my* daddy. In my eyes, *he* was love.

I guess the confusion and wreckage began the day I opened the door to his truck and a playing card fell out. I picked it up to stuff it back into the black plastic bag it had fallen from behind the passenger seat. But when I turned it over I saw the picture of a naked woman. And a man. Doing things I certainly didn't understand.

Then there was the night I tiptoed downstairs to get a late-night snack and instead turned the corner to see my dad on the couch watching TV. And the images on the screen made my heart feel dirty for even seeing. And the countless times I'd walk into the home office and catch him quickly turning off the computer screen.

Pornography.

It was dirty. Confusing for a child to see.

I didn't know at the time what a stronghold it held over my father's life. Every piece of me prayed my mommy didn't know. Oh, how I hoped my mommy didn't know. It was disturbing and filthy. But the most confusing thing to me was that when I'd innocently stumble in on my dad's struggle, *I* was the one who would get in trouble.

His clenched jaw and stern eyes and embarrassed, flustered look almost demanded silence. I was made to feel guilty. Suddenly another's sins became my shame. I realized the daddy I loved was full of broken things.

The older I became the harder he became to read. Sometimes I'd walk in on him reading his Bible and other times I'd catch him watching porn. There were times he would lead our family in prayer and other times I'd peek during prayer to see him staring at the football game on TV in the background. There were times I'd see him help the weak and love on the poor, and other times I'd see him waste hours on the couch while my mom worked tirelessly to meet our needs.

It was confusing, really. To love a man so fiercely but see apathy weave through his days. To see a man as your hero but question his faithfulness in many ways.

But every time he fell short and I noticed, I was the one who was punished. And everything in me *hated* failing my father. My stomach would sink when I knew he was disappointed and I learned quickly that the good things I did would bring attention and praise and the things I did wrong, which always seemed to change, brought condemnation and shame.

So I set my mind to working hard to please my earthly father. Cracks crept into my foundational understanding of what love really was. My interpretation of love became a balancing act and my interpretation of God's love followed suit.

## The Pursuit of Perfection

With each passing year, the strangleholds of my dad's struggles seemed to grip tighter at his peace. They seemed to slowly rob him of that infectious ease that once strung through his soft Southern drawl. He became more irritable. And quick-tempered. The list of things that would set him off grew. A house that used to echo with the pitter-patter of love-drunk feet felt more like a house made of glass.

In my preteen years, I often felt like I was walking on eggshells around the dad I desired so desperately to please. When things were good, they were wonderful. Our family made memories filled with laughter.

But when things were off, they were increasingly hard to read.

My dominant personality didn't help the situation. If I was bullheaded as a child I was brazen as a young teen. My patience-testing and boundary-pushing and norm-challenging ways took a toll on parents who I'm sure would have loved a little rest. But at the core of my heart, I was still their baby girl—who ached with every ounce of myself to make them proud.

What became challenging was that the stern stare and tightened jaw I would receive from my dad when I'd done something wrong evolved into daylong silent treatments. And the list of "wrongs" seemed to constantly grow and become even more subjective to the mood he was in. Academically, perfection was expected. It was guaranteed that if we brought home a B there would be a scolding. Athletically, the standard was no different. The sport I loved at times flirted with becoming the sport I played just to make my father happy.

There were too many soccer games to count where I would make a poor play or allow a soft goal and tremble as I peeked over at the sidelines. If his arms were crossed and his legs were spread, I knew the car ride home would be silent. On the flip side, when I excelled I was suddenly back in the passenger seat as "daddy's best girl." When we won big games or I made great plays, our car rides were filled with vivid accounts of the victory and laughing and cheering and ice cream stops before we headed for home.

A part of me understood it—a parent's desire for the best from their child. An expectation of perfection because they know "better and best" are somewhere down deep, past the blood and the sweat and the tears. I really didn't blame my dad. It all seemed like an emotional rollercoaster, but in many ways I appreciated how hard he pushed me. I was a stubborn teen who *needed* pushing. But the problem that was building was a problem we all face when we exalt wrecked idols and anxiously await their affirmation and praise. We come to the conclusion that *love* is works-based. That when we do the wrong things we are loved less. And when we do the right things we are loved more. Our concept of unconditional love actually feels a lot like conditional love—with the conditions being our work, our abilities, our failures, and our strength. What's most dangerous about our picture of love being painted around such a deceitful mentality is that our perception of God's love for us mirrors it. We're too preoccupied with winning favor to hear that it's not the same type of love in God's economy.

My fixation on winning the favor of a fickle father owned me. Perfectionism poured from me. A thirst for success led me as I set my eyes on a transition I'd been anxiously waiting to step into for a while.

High school.

A new opportunity to be an even *better me*.

# 3

# Watch Me Work

There were a number of things I wanted to control. We've all known that feeling, haven't we?

I had always been a dominant personality. That was nothing new. Any tangible control I could have over something, I relished. I was the type of girl who kept my middle school locker religiously organized, who practiced perfect penmanship with my right *and* left hands, who orchestrated the games at recess and assigned nonnegotiable roles for each person playing. I was a force. An expert at the art of subtle manipulation—using my size or my charm or my words to get my way.

A natural-born leader, they would say. Maybe. But also naturally stubborn and fiercely self-willed. I had a drive and desire to dictate my success that was far beyond my years. It was a characteristic that would serve me well in some ways, once molded over time, but proved to cause more alienation than achievement when I was young.

It's not that the shift from middle school to high school was some type of radical transition. But it was a *transition*. And with a change in surroundings came the opportunity to control several new things. It seems like the transitions in life—the times where so much is so unpredictable and so little is truly in our control—are often the times we crave control the most. Where we become most restless and self-focused. This shift in my life was no exception.

I feel like that longing for control is woven through each of us. Control over *something*. Anything. It's engrained in us. A deep desire for autonomy and ownership. An overwhelming responsibility to claim possession of our own lives.

We're told that's what marks a successful life in our society. The self-made millionaire. The rags-to-riches story fueled by *self*-control and *personal* strength and *individual* willpower. Maybe, just maybe, if we can control enough in our lives we can map our own course. And maybe, if we're good enough, that course will lead to the life we planned for ourselves. To success. And excess. And worth.

Maybe if we can singlehandedly control where all the cards fall, we can live up to the world's expectation of us. To our parents' expectation of us. To our own expectation of us.

Maybe.

Or maybe, just maybe, we're missing the point.

## My Predetermined Plans

I was entering high school wide-eyed and success-driven. With newfound freedoms came newfound goals. There were so many components of my life that I had predetermined were going to look a certain way.

Athletically, soccer was at the foundation of my identity. Not only was it a pursuit of mine sure to garner my dad's attention and praise but it was also a pursuit I knew, beyond a shadow of a doubt, I was naturally gifted in. Soccer was *my thing*—it always had been. From the first time I slid on a pair of goalkeeper gloves there was an instinctual awareness and a raw talent that I wore like badges of honor. There was also a strong work ethic to back it up and an ego-driven thirst to be the best.

I was on the State Olympic Development team at the time. I had goals to make the Regional Olympic Team, the US National Team for my age group, in order to garner a college scholarship. I wanted to make the varsity high school team as a freshman and really wasn't planning on settling for anything less than what my arrogance had deemed possible. I had made a name for myself in the soccer community up until that point. And now, with colleges watching and more notoriety on the line, it was time to show up and show out.

At the same time, I desired greater control over another extracurricular interest of mine—entertainment. I had grown up dabbling in professional acting and radio work. From working as the first Atlanta Radio Disney Kid Correspondent, to being named the "Youngest Sportscaster in America" and cohosting my own sports-talk radio show on AM 790 The Zone, to shooting a nationally run television commercial and various video series, I was no stranger to microphones and cameras. I had always been comfortable in an audition room with a panel of casting directors. Auditioning for movies like *Remember the Titans* and television shows like *Lizzie McGuire*, I had marked my adolescence with a bold confidence and a fearless, if somewhat oblivious, mentality regarding the pressures and scrutiny of the entertainment industry.

But as I moved into high school and began to mature physically, the dynamic of the industry seemed to waste no time in raising the bar toward new and different expectations. My mind also seemed to waste no time in desiring to control my entertainment-related success in a new way. Fun commercial auditions evolved into meatier, more involved roles that were few and far between if I didn't possess the right "look." Silly radio auditions evolved into in-person "cattle calls" at a prestigious modeling agency. Playful video shoots evolved into the world of beauty pageants, swimsuits, gowns, and more scrutiny. I yearned to control my success in every avenue of entertainment—if not for the money, then for the recognition. Where soccer was my daddy-daughter lifeline, pageants and performance were my mom's and my playing fields. The perfectionist in me longed to be equally successful in everything I did.

Relationships were another piece of the puzzle I wanted to dictate. It was no mystery that my relationship with my dad was constantly in flux. Still consumed by achievements warranting his praise and failures inviting his frustration and silence, I wanted this new chapter of my life to turn a page on the tension of our past and bring some stability. I wanted to control how our relationship would continue to play out and I, idealistically, wanted to be able to control my success to the point that he would never have reason to be disappointed or angry with me again.

I also had a deep desire to control how my friendships played out, as well as how boys perceived me. Coming into my own and trying to navigate maturity, I was starting to focus heavily on the praise and attention I could get from boys. High school boys seemed so different from middle school boys. I had been much taller than most of the boys in middle school and was looking forward to stepping into high school and garnering the attention I knew I was bound to naturally receive as a new freshman on campus. It was important to me—to my worth and to my self-confidence—that I be a topic of conversation with the guys. That I be somewhat envied and looked up to by the girls. What young girl doesn't desire to be praised and affirmed and wanted? It's half the reason we take so long to get ready in the mornings. It's part of why we learn how to do our hair, how to dress well, and how to paint our faces with makeup. Deep down, young girls—even self-proclaimed tomboys—desire to feel beautiful. At that age, the eyes and attention of peers seem to be the clearest gauge of that worth.

But above all, I wanted control socially. When I stepped into high school, I wanted to be able to determine who I would connect with, where I would fit in, and what social group I would be a part of. The transition held so many unknowns because each new freshman class was made up of chunks of students from several different middle schools merging together. Add all of the older and more experienced upper classmen into the mix, and it made the social scene as intimidating as it was unpredictable. It's not that I foresaw myself being the *most* popular girl in school, but I hoped to be accepted by the popular crowd. Whoever the "popular crowd" was supposed to be. It was important to me that I socially "fit." After all, I was a confident and competent girl. I had athletic gifts, an impressive entertainment résumé, and an outgoing personality. In my mind, I was primed to move into high school with ease and control. My security was built on my assumption that my predetermined plans would play out exactly as I'd prepared. My identity hung in the balance of my strength, my discipline, and my control.

I paid little regard to my faith. I was comfortable. Comfortable with the cultural Christianity I'd walked through for years. Comfortable with claiming the title, praying when it was convenient, and talking the talk along the way. The faith walk I knew hadn't proven to be anything less than *enough* yet, so any intentionality or focus on growing my faith as I transitioned into this new season of life was an afterthought. In fact, the only subconscious mindset I had surrounding any component of faith was simple—*God, watch me work.*

It wasn't that I turned my back on God but rather that I turned all of my focus toward myself. My work, my goals, my plans, my success. In fact, I often rationalized that since apparently God had set the stage for me in many regards, it was now my responsibility to perform on that stage and succeed. I was convinced that my *own* personal strength and internal drive were solely responsible for controlling the outcome of my story, and my pride moved God to the back burner, placing a weight far greater than I could bear on my own two shoulders.

## Captivated by Control

It wasn't long before my hunger for control left me unexpectedly starved. When I did finally enter high school, I quickly realized I had little control over anything at all. And I most clearly lacked control over the things that were the most important to me at the time.

There were girls on the soccer field who were stronger, better, and faster than I was. There were girls in the Olympic Development Program advancing through the ranks of teams faster than I could keep up with—surpassing their state teams and moving on to Regional Olympic teams, National Olympic camps, and international competitions. While I was still a top-ranking player within my age group, I couldn't help but covet the promotion and success of the other top players around me. I was constantly tuned in to what colleges they were hearing from, who was playing where, and what the coaches were saying about different positional players and goalkeepers.

My dad stayed tuned in to all of the updates and newsworthy sideline talk as well. And while he certainly never made me feel less than capable of working my way to the top, I couldn't help but grow anxious about what he might be thinking, what more I could be doing to impress him, and how I could make him as proud as possible. His hopes for my future seemed as insatiable as my desperate desire to make that future a reality.

As college coaches began attending my games, I felt an added pressure to perform perfectly. As recruiters filled the Olympic training camps, my mind became more occupied with assessing who was watching and wondering what they were thinking than focused on the game and enjoying the experience. I became fixated with seeing to it that I was constantly making an impression. Obsessed with wondering if my name was on the coaches' lips. Consumed with analyzing my performance post-game—the things I did right, the things I did wrong, what people may have thought. In my desperation for control, I was losing control—and losing perspective on the purpose of even playing the sport.

On the entertainment side of things, my controlling and overanalytical mind invited me down another disjointed path. With fewer and fewer auditions coming in as my casting demographic shifted to an older, more developed range, I was already wrestling with insecurity surrounding my "look" and my potential future in the industry. According to casting directors, my look was too exotic to be commercial and too commercial to be exotic. I was too tall to be cast for younger roles and too young-looking to pass for roles that would warrant my height. I was too athletically built to be cast next to smaller boys but not athletically built enough to be used for fitness-specific jobs. In summary, I was stuck in no-man's-land and felt, most of the time, like I simply wasn't *enough* of any one thing to be successful. Which felt, most days, like *I* wasn't enough. At all.

Pageants were a whole new ballgame, but one that ran in my blood. My mom, after all, had been a pageant queen multiple times. She held four crowns through her youth and placed third-runner-up to Miss Alabama in 1979. While she attended Troy State University on a leadership scholarship through the Girls State program, her scholarship was financially supplemented by pageant money she'd won as well. I wanted, desperately, to be as successful as my mommy had been in a field she enjoyed so much.

I'll never forget the day I sat at an interview table with a Miss Georgia Teen USA pageant judge. We had completed pre-judging for the swimsuit portion of the competition earlier that day for the same panel of judges, and I had walked as tall and as proud as any fifteen-year-old in that convention center. With two swatches of fabric covering my body and the required three-inch heels strapped to my feet, I had mustered the bravery to flaunt my muscular, athletic physique with as much pride as I knew how. On the stage I felt confident and beautiful and *in control*. But for whatever reason, sitting in that chair, with the undivided attention of a judge just a few feet away, my mind sprinted through what he might be thinking.

*Does he like me? Does he remember me from the swimsuit pre-judging? Did I make an impression?*

"You're bio says you're an athlete," he said as he stared at me with as blank an expression as I'd ever seen.

*Is that an advantage for me? Is he saying that in a favorable way? Has a competitive athlete ever won this pageant?*

"Yes, I am! I've been playing soccer for most of my life. I'm a goalkeeper and I compete on the Olympic Development team for our state," I replied. Still trying to read his blank, unfazed expression, I worked to ease the pressure of the moment with more words. "It's very fun. A lot of running, a lot of diving around the net to make saves. It certainly helps put on plenty of muscle!"

Before I could sling a smile across my face, his next words caught me so off-guard I've never forgotten the moment. With bulging eyes, he scanned my body up and down as I sat in my ironed interview suit and simply said in a very condescending tone, "I was at the swimsuit judging. Trust me, *I could tell.*"

And with those few words, a piercing eye-roll, and a few unknown notes written down on his evaluation sheet, I wanted nothing more than to sink into my chair and disappear from the room. I remember feeling, for the very first time, like there was something wrong with my body. Sure, I had always wrestled with some insecurity about my height, but that was nothing I could control. Now, sitting in front of an adult—an adult experienced in judging and evaluating a certain standard of physical beauty—I felt I was inadequate. And as a fifteen-year-old girl I first began to truly believe the lie that I didn't measure up. That my body wasn't good enough.

And, with that, another layer of control slipped from my grasp.

Control over the relationships in my life seemed to slide from my grip just as quickly. At home, my dad's moods were becoming increasingly unpredictable. Where I had desired, so deeply, to tread carefully in his wake and keep the peace and stability between us, I had quickly fallen short. Between his demanding expectations of my grades, athletic performances, and obedience and my stubborn personality, resentment toward his pornography struggles and laziness, and brazen disobedience in an effort to navigate the changing hormones that came along with maturity and growth, the tension was always unpredictable in our house. Some days we were inseparable, bound at the hip and running all around town together. Other days we were passive-aggressive and temperamental.

As much as my dad thrived in raising my sister and me as young kids, he struggled in raising us as teenage girls. I can't say that I blame him. I was challenging to love. I was busy building grand plans for the course of my days in the sand of pride and praise while he was wrestling the pressures of providing for a fast-paced family, the difficulty of self-employment, and the emotional struggles and fixations he was a bit too prideful to acknowledge. We were so similar. Emotional and passionate. Stubborn and strong-willed. Dominant and controlling. As we wrestled for that relational control, we both seemed to lose it. And the casualties of that battle usually involved our hearts.

The final thread of control I clung to so tightly wasted no time in unraveling. Socially, my journey looked nothing like I'd planned. I walked into high school at six feet tall and 165 pounds. I think I made it around a corner and past one set of lockers on the first day of school before I heard the first "Giant!" remark, coupled with some laughs and stares. "That's a biiiiig b**ch," followed suit and, "Look at that *huge* girl!"

seemed to quickly trail behind. If these whispered comments weren't enough, the fact that I didn't know a single person from any of the converging middle schools didn't help. Many of my friends from my middle school seemed to already know and have established friend groups with kids from the other districts, but since soccer had always consumed most of my free time I'd never crossed paths with the majority of the teens in my freshman class.

I longed to fit in with the popular group that was clearly forming, but no matter how hard I tried I always seemed to sit right on the outside. I was an acquaintance but not a close friend tied to any one group. I was the girl who people would hang with at school but never invite to the get-togethers on the weekends. Or if I was, my soccer commitments always conflicted. So eventually the phone stopped ringing.

I wasn't one of the girls all of the boys swooned over—I didn't have all the newest fashions or know all the trends. I didn't care to get dressed to the nines every day for school. I didn't carry the absurd handbags some of the most well-liked girls toted around. I didn't drive the Mercedes so many teens somehow whipped into our high school parking lot. I wasn't the most beautiful, I wasn't the most socially connected, and I wasn't made to feel welcome by the upperclassmen like so many of the other freshmen seemed to be.

I was just *me*. I tried, for a long time, to fit the mold of what seemed to be so well liked. I tried to stay in with the gossip of all that was going on and tried to make sure I was sitting with the right people in class and seen with the right people in the halls. I tried to hide my height and find my clique and blend with the social scene. But at the end of the day I was left feeling out of control and ultimately just not good enough.

## Identity Crisis

We are creatures made to worship. But when we turn our focus from worshiping the Creator who made us to worshiping the blessings He's given us, we construct self-made standards we force ourselves to live up to through our own strength and ability. It's like praising the soccer ball for scoring a goal rather than acknowledging the coach who trained you how to properly kick it. It's easy for our gifts or our talents or our skills to falsely shape part of our identity. And it's easy to disappoint ourselves when we move through life with an identity rooted in such unidentifiable things. And, for some reason, we seem to be people who would rather place our hope in manmade autonomy than surrender our lives to a God-designed identity when that identity requires faith to believe.

My biggest issue with certain things not playing out as I'd hoped was that I saw those same things as foundational to my identity. The wreckage that seemed to come wasn't just wreckage of my plans or my success, it was wreckage of my self-concept. In my hope to control each thing perfectly, I was ultimately desperate to control my own emotional and mental construct of *me*. At that time, I needed something, anything, to be *my thing*.

I craved ownership and autonomy so deeply that I was willing to do anything to find something to worship freely. The plans I'd built in the sand of pride and praise were sliding. The course I'd planned to walk was weaving and widening. As the control I craved slipped through my fingers, I did exactly what our anxious human nature convinces us we must do—I blindly strained and grasped for more.

# 4

# A House of Mirrors

It was in my desperate thirst for control that I first heard the enemy's quenching lies. If there was one fundamental thing I had actually listened to and learned in church it was that there was an enemy. I guess what I didn't fully understand was how keen and sly that enemy was, and how easily I could be deceived. What began as lending an ear to the curious thoughts of what I could still control developed into a spiritual illness that owned my manic days.

It wasn't as if my wrecked fixation developed overnight—eating disorders never do. No, it was much more gradual than that, like a stew slowly coming to a boil. The ingredients were all there: lies I believed from my past, frustration and control issues in the present, insecurities and anxiety about the future. It all began as a slow simmer—a *need* for ownership over something. Before I knew it, my obsession boiled over and burned every aspect of my life.

## Liar, Liar

If God is said to speak in a still, small voice, then Satan's wrecking words are like guttural screams through a megaphone. They were all I could hear, and they grew louder and louder with each passing day.

*Failure.*

*Fraud.*

*Not beautiful enough.*

*Not talented enough.*

*Not smart enough.*

*Too big.*

*Too thick.*

*Too different.*

For a while I had enough fight in me to ignore them. After all, I lived a blessed life full of potential and provision. All of my needs were met and I was well loved. I had my health, my education, opportunity. On paper, I should have been the girl who was strong enough and well enough off to pull herself up by her bootstraps and press on. I even felt guilty, at times, when the lies rang through my thoughts and I allowed them to dent and scratch my blessed armor. I had known a youth full of affirmation and encouragement and achievement. I shouldn't have been the one wrestling with these things. I wasn't that kind of lonely, broken girl. I was *me*.

But Satan never discriminates when he targets and teases. He could care less about who I was. What he always sees first is easy targets in the unguarded weak. Even with all the support in the world around us—an armor built thick and sturdy through our own personal strength—it takes the supernatural equipment of a King who's already won the war to stand a chance in the personal attacks and battles of the enemy's deceit.

*Confident? Capable? You're not even strong enough to control the few things you planned to.*

*Look around you. Where do you even fit? You have tension in your home, you have tension with your teammates, you have tension in the school's social scene.*

*You're so desperate—pining for things you'll never achieve.*

*You'll never have control over something because you're too weak to sacrifice anything.*

*You're just too weak.*

The constant words grew in such intensity and frequency that eventually I came to believe they were my own thoughts. They disguised themselves as the brutally honest voice inside of me and I began to adopt them as my own insecurities. In the times I would allow my mind to wander, it always seemed to return with new lies from the enemy. Lies I began to allow to sculpt me—to reshape my worth, my confidence, my stability.

I became fixated with my own insecurities and obsessed with my weaknesses and failings. No matter how many successes or positives surrounded me, I was colorblind to the hues of their beauty. Negative thoughts stole my joy and dragged me back into the gray area of uncertainty. With each new thought I failed to take captive and let wander like an intruder within me, it was like another mirror rose up around me, and before I knew it I felt like I was in a house of mirrors. Surrounded on all sides by a warped reflection of myself, all I could see was me. My life, my wants, my flesh, my needs. My failures, my inadequacies, my discomfort, my insecurities.

I think it's one of the enemy's greatest tactics, really. To provoke us to becoming so fixated with our own thoughts and wants that we are blind to the world around us. If we're being honest, it doesn't take much to coax us into a house of mirrors by making us believe that we are solely responsible for controlling our own lives—and that we must do it perfectly. These lies take us by the hand and walk us into a maze of self-obsession and self-absorption where all we can see is ourselves. They lure us away from a healthy perspective of the world around us and invite us into an all-consuming isolation that is blind to reality. How can we possibly see clearly, much less set our eyes on anything greater, when we are surrounded by mirrors that only ever reflect our own skewed needs?

*There is something you **can** control.*

That taunt came as swiftly as a second breath from the lips of deceit. It's never enough to simply torment our heads and our hearts—Satan always takes it a step further and disguises a lie as a tempting reprieve from the suffering. And as much as I knew it was wrong, the thought of finding something—anything—to be *my thing* was appetizing. I hadn't lost my taste for control, just my will to stand uncompromised morally.

*Of all things, you can control your body.*

*You don't have to be the huge girl. The giant.*

*Taking control of your body would help with everything: athletically, in entertainment, socially.*

*All of the ways you fall short revolve around your body.*

*And it's yours, after all. So do with it what you please.*

There was something enticing about the shards of broken truth that framed that self-centered lie. It was *my* body. And, of all things, that was something nobody else had more exclusive access to than me. If I could better control my body, I could force it to fit a mold more suited to the things I wanted to achieve. Sure, it might be uncomfortable at times. Nobody said the process of control was pretty. But I had the tendencies of an athlete ingrained in me and I was used to pushing myself past my comfort zone to achieve what others couldn't do for me. If I ever wanted to gain anything, I had to be willing to sacrifice something. Whatever that may be. If anyone was going to suffer from the sacrifice I needed to make, it might as well be me.

That was where my illness began. From the toxin of lies came the self-prescribed antidote of compromise. What eventually grew out of that was a vigilante attitude of controlling my life and my body to such an extreme degree that nobody else would have any reason to be disappointed in me or think less of me. If I could control my body, I could control something. And if that control ultimately benefitted me, then it was worth whatever sacrifice or discomfort it brought me. Nobody would have to know. No, this would be my thing. If I could hide the struggle well enough, it would make the success that followed seem as though it came naturally. That perception of ease was important to me—to my ego, my pride, and my deeply insecure need for praise and worth and affirmation.

I had already been exposed to so many things that served to reinforce the lie that my body defined my worth. Pornography. Movies. Magazines. Advertisements. TV. It was impossible to go anywhere without some cultural reinforcement that a woman's true power and value came from her exterior beauty. It wasn't just national media reinforcing that message—I had a face-to-face reminder of it every single day as I walked through the halls at school. The most popular and well-liked girls always seemed to be well-toned, well-developed, well-tanned, and impeccably dressed. Their beauty was coveted and gawked at and chased and praised by girls and guys alike. It seemed to come with the territory—a requirement of sorts—that to "fit" with the most popular crowd, your beauty had to precede you. Or the "beauty" trending that semester, at least. To a girl who longed to have all that she didn't, that power was worth compromising *anything*. So, with all things considered, I stepped further into my house of mirrors and wandered deeper into my disoriented suffering.

## Losing Control

It's not as though I spent my first days hunched over a toilet with my fingers down my throat and bloodshot eyes. No, my struggles began much more subtly than that. It began as daily, cognizant decisions to control the small choices. I watched what foods I picked to eat and the size of my portions. I watched how frequently I was exercising or how much energy I'd seemed to have exerted at soccer practice. My habit of eating larger portions was hard to break, but there was something in the hunger pains that soothed me.

I started to feel better if I was acutely aware that my body was aching for more. In my mind, if my body was always slightly hungry, then that was a sure sign I was never overindulging. If I wasn't overindulging, then my body was being forced to burn away some of the stored fuel and fat I was carrying. When I didn't feel like I had burned enough calories at practice, I would tag an extra workout onto that day's schedule. Small equations always seemed to creep into my mind, balancing out what I had eaten and what I suspected I'd burned off. The hunger pains weren't ideal, but they were manageable. I reveled in managing them closely. It was comforting to know that I was controlling my will. Craving but not caving in to what my body and brain desperately needed.

Eventually, the rush I got from controlling my hunger and seeing the slow changes in my body coaxed me to even more drastic extremes. Not only was I watching, more religiously, the types and amounts of foods I was eating but I also began to watch people around me make their food choices. Observation turned to comparison and comparison turned to judgment. I was oddly jealous of those around me who seemingly had the willpower to make more disciplined, constraining food choices than I did and oddly resentful of those who seemed to pay no mind to what they consumed. Perhaps a part of me longed for their freedom—but a bigger part of me grew in silent bitterness and disdain for those who were weaker and less disciplined than I was learning how to be.

My changed behavior seemed to only tighten the tension at home with my dad. Food was his vice. That was no mystery. For a man who found great comfort and enjoyment in eating, my newfound nibbling seemed to frustrate him to no end. My attitude toward his excessive eating didn't help, and the deeper I sunk into my disorder the more expressive I became in my judgment of his choices.

My competitive nature only seemed to fuel my issues. I was developing an unhealthy relationship with food, one that first grew out of an unhealthy relationship with my own body. Which first grew out of an unhealthy relationship with my body's own Creator. That relationship was as starved and aching as my shrinking frame.

My hunger pains were gripping and my headaches were increasing and fatigue was always present. But if I could ignore the pain in my growling stomach long enough to fall asleep at night, the rush of success I would feel the next morning made the new day's battle seem worth it.

Desperate for even more control, I began a daily log. Whatever I ate, I wrote down. Every physical activity or workout or practice, I charted. I became fixated with the numbers and indulged in equations to keep track of my discipline: calories consumed minus calories burned. Every day was a new competition. Defeating each hunger pain was a small battle won, and making it through an entire day without cracking or caving was the ultimate victory. The smaller the resulting numbers became in the equations, the larger my pride and my sense of control grew. I rationalized that I was simply a health-conscious eater—I was a competitor and an athlete, and all great champions made sacrifices in their strides toward greatness.

But as my body struggled, my athletic performance followed suit. When my lack of energy caught up with me in training sessions and I couldn't quite push through like I used to, my anxious emotional state became even more fragile. Fragile enough that, finally, one day biology overrode my will and I spiraled even further out of control.

I can remember all of the mental and emotional torment so clearly. I cracked. And binged. Standing in the narrow pantry of my childhood home, I ate and I ate and I ate. My stomach cramped and ached in shock, but I just couldn't stop. I ate anything I could get my hands on until I'd scraped that pantry empty—and then I moved to the fridge. My mind went numb as I gorged myself with food and mentally satiated every nagging hunger pain I'd wrestled with for months. In the moment it was euphoric. Like an addict finally getting a long-awaited fix, I reveled in the food-induced high. But it didn't take long, once I finally slowed to a stop, for the high to fade and my thoughts to creep back as I sat bloated and defeated and wracked with self-disgust.

*Fat.*

*Glutton.*

*You weak, weak woman.*

54

*You'll be just as fat as you ever were.*

*All that you've sacrificed and all that you've worked for is lost.*

*You thought you had control? You're pathetic.*

*You can't control a thing. You failed. You slob.*

*You'll end up looking just like your father—his size is in your genes, after all.*

*If you don't make this right, you'll never be good enough.*

Satan's adaptability to the specifics of our circumstance is unrelenting. I couldn't win. The lies would appear one way for one season of thought and morph into another way for the next. There was never a moment of reprieve. It's as if the enemy is bitter that he doesn't have the power to *create* or bring life, like the King of all kings, and his only hope is in his ability to copy or mimic or camouflage himself in the midst of our suffering. If we're not aware of this tactic and prepared for this strategy, it becomes so easy to believe anything and everything.

The next thing I knew my legs were dragging me upstairs to the privacy of the jack-and-jill bathroom I shared with my sister. As if my body had a will of its own, I anxiously locked the door and rounded the corner behind the small knee-wall and hunched my tear-filled face over the shining toilet bowl.

*Get yourself together. Stop crying over a problem you brought on yourself.*

*You know what you have to do. If you don't, every one of those calories will destroy you.*

*They'll destroy your progress, your body, your beauty.*

*Think of all the things you want.*

*You lost control for a moment. Now gain it back.*

*You know what you have to do. You can do it. I'm here for you.*

My hand trembled by my mouth as my last thread of responsibility and rationality fought to win this moment in my story. I didn't have to do this. I wasn't that girl. Girls who made themselves throw up had eating disorders. Certainly I wasn't that weak. I tried to convince myself I could burn off the calories and get right back to watching what I ate and taking control of my intake. I tried to convince myself I knew better than this—to snap out of this twisted picture. But the house of mirrors around me seemed to sing a different tune, and before I knew it I was rationalizing my anxiousness away and reaching as deep into my throat as my fingers could.

It wasn't easy. The back of my throat felt sharp and sensitive and I had to shake my fingers around for my gag reflex to finally respond with an aggressive move. But after a moment of struggling I felt a thick, clogged warmth roll up my throat and my eyes streamed tears and my face felt like the pressure might make it explode. But there it came. All of my regret and anxiety rolled up out of my throat and splashed into the empty bowl. Again and again and again I pried until my body would toss up more food. The thickness of the half-chewed failure ached my throat and the pressure of the convulsions caused blood vessels in my eyes to burst. Finally, the sour burning of the stomach acid that was left stung my tongue and I stopped, exhausted, and cried. By the time I lifted my head and looked into the mirror my face was as red as my bloodshot eyes. Mascara streamed down my nose and splatters of vomit covered my cheeks. I sat down against the pale blue walls of my childhood bathroom and, between my confusion and self-disgust, stared into the full toilet and sighed in overwhelming relief. There it was. All I needed to see. As splattered and filthy and tearstained as it was, it was the regaining of my control. The wreckage felt like victory.

## Will You See Me?

My anorexia had evolved into bulimia and my dark ownership of my body was nothing I talked about. It was simpler for a while. Binging and purging was a habit far easier to maintain than eating nothing at all. The discomfort wasn't completely gone—hunger pains were simply replaced by an aching throat and a raw mouth from stomach acid purged out the wrong way. But I found a rhythm in my habit. I started to become bolder in where and how frequently I would find my way to a toilet to feel some control.

*You know, you could be doing more.*

*If you want more, you need to be willing to give more.*

*You have some control now, why not strive for more?*

*Take more. Do more. Be better.*

Upward of ten times a day—that's how often I found myself leaning over a toilet bowl or washing chunks of food down the shower drain or wiping my quivering, burning mouth. In my effort to control even more, my binging gradually evolved back to nibbling—even as I kept purging. Some days I would eat as little as an apple and purge shortly after. When my fingers could no longer stimulate my gag reflex, I started using objects. A toothbrush, the base of a hair brush, anything that would force me to vomit. Anything to get those calories out.

Eventually, my body became so accustomed to pushing the food back up that I found I couldn't even keep food down. I had conditioned my body to purge almost immediately—which would have been ideal had it not made hiding my secret tougher. I found myself fighting to stay seated at the dinner table long enough to dismiss myself rather than rushing off to the bathroom. Even when the little I'd eaten did roll back up, I'd choke it back and try to wait it out. Half of me was constantly nervous my parents were aware, and the other half of me was fiercely protective of the secret I refused to share.

The calories my brain convinced me I still needed to burn had to be handled somehow. With my soccer career progressing and my desperate desire to continue excelling athletically, exercise became an absolute obsession. Summer found me working out close to six hours a day. Religiously, obsessively, I trained. Running constantly, lifting weights, sprinting stadiums, then repeating it all over again. With no fuel left in me, I turned to the next level of compromise—pills. Any dietary pill I could possibly take that would provide me with synthetic energy, I took. I moved through the entire display of fat-burning promises and muscle-building quick-fixes and energy-packed supplements that lined the drugstore shelves. I rationalized that I was focused and improving for my sport, but the truth was that success in the sport, at that point, was secondary to success in controlling my body—a welcome by-product of my fixation, but no longer my motivating factor. My identity was owned by something different, something far more sinister than my goals and my successful feats. My identity was owned by a spiritual illness and physical disease that was slowly destroying me.

I was obsessed. All-consumed. Methodical. A servant to any and every lie Satan sold and a victim of every twisted truth my mind perceived. The enemy refused to leave me be. No part of me had any energy left to fight the manic behavior that owned me. My mind could always whip up a fresh rationalization— one of a thousand reasons why my secret and my habits were helpful and beneficial and good. I had a new excuse for my fatigued heart every day. I was weak and broken and hurting

and strained. But on the outside it looked as though I was suc-
ceeding in every way.

―――――――――――

Through all of the pain, the abuse of my body, the neglect
and obsession, the lies and fixations, I found myself finally suc-
ceeding by society's norms. In the midst of my mess, athletically
I was excelling tremendously. I was finally selected onto the
Regional Olympic Soccer team and began competing interna-
tionally in Sweden, Mexico, Germany, Austria, and Italy. In 2006
I was named a youth All-American by the Soccer Coaches As-
sociation of America. In 2007 I was named the Atlanta Journal
Constitution Player of the Year. I broke every goalkeeping record
at Lassiter High School and was finally invited to US National
team training camps. On the entertainment side of things I
won and placed in beauty pageants, including placing Top 15
in Miss Georgia Teen USA. I began fielding interest and pursuit
from countless universities, and eventually signed a Division I
college scholarship to LSU. I fielded new compliments of "how
gorgeous" I looked, and garnered a one-on-one meeting with
an executive at a prestigious international modeling agency.
Relationally, I was suddenly becoming a person of interest in my
high school halls and capturing the attention of the boys both
in my grade and upperclassmen alike. And socially, I was suddenly finding myself more accepted and worthy of the popular
crowd's attention and time.

All I had hoped to control was laid out before me. And
every part of me truly believed that once I'd achieved these
things I would be happy. Every person I met reminded me,
looking at my incredible circumstances, that I was so lucky. Yet

standing in the success of my self-centered sacrifice, all I felt was *empty*.

I suppose we always figure that the benefits will outweigh the costs. We wouldn't yearn for control or believe the countless lies or be more than willing to compromise if we didn't truly believe it would all be worth something in the end. We begin with the end goal in mind. Then somewhere along the way the motivating factor shifts to become our pride. Scripture warns us that pride comes before a fall. Yet every time we lay in our own wreckage after the fall and wonder why we feel nothing at all. We think we know best what we want and what we need, yet our chapter of wreckage always ends in a slow bleed. And when we realize that what we thought we needed doesn't satisfy, we crawl, in shame, back to the starting line.

———————

There was never a specific moment where I stared myself down, acknowledged the severity of my eating disorder, and declared that it had to stop. I'm not sure I believed I could stop. I knew that I was sick and fiercely tired and desperate for some type of break. But I'm not sure I ever believed that was fully possible for me. After all, I knew my demons for three and a half years. I moved through all of high school wrestling lies and obsessions and rationalizations and fixations. My house of mirrors was my home. As mentally and emotionally and spiritually exhausted as I was, I had grown familiar with only ever seeing my own reflection. In a sick way, I felt safe in my condition.

But at some point toward the end of my time in high school I stumbled across a piece of Scripture that simply read, "Come to me, all you who are weary and burdened, and I will give you rest" (Matt. 11:28). I was set to graduate a semester early and head off to Louisiana State University to begin training with the soccer team in the spring and, for whatever reason, something in this tiny verse stirred something fierce inside of me. Aching and ill and dying for the promised rest, I turned for just a moment from my disease and found my way to my knees.

My prayer was nothing fancy. It was cloaked in shame and frustration and apprehension. My words were desperate and raw and nothing I'd be proud to repeat. But they were all I could find in the midst of my suffering, and much to my surprise at the time, God's grace gently found me.

*God, I can't do this anymore. "Come to me, all who are weary and burdened, and I will give you rest." If that's true, will you see me? I've tried so hard to control so many things. And I'm terrible at it. I'm tired. And I'm hurting. And I want nothing more than to be set free. If that's even possible . . . will you see me, God? Will you see me?*

It's hard to describe the courage that flooded me—the strength that found me in that blue-carpeted bedroom in our house at the end of our quiet street. I felt *peace*. And even though my hands still trembled and I had no idea what my next step was supposed to be, I knew, deep in my heart, there *was* a next step for me. I suppose I was gifted hope that night—a tiny breath of hope that healing was possible and that this bondage didn't have the power to own me. Hope that there was something more than the shame of my suffering.

A few moments later my mom walked into my bedroom to put away some laundry. My hands were sweating profusely and my heart was pounding, and once more I allowed the hot bulge in my throat to billow out of me. This time it wasn't food I was releasing, it was truth—and it poured from me. I opened up to my mom about everything I had been doing, everything I had been hiding, and all of the damage I'd wreaked on my body and my heart for the past several years. I half-expected anger and frustration to well up within her, but was shocked when her tears met mine and a holy anguish flowed from her like grace and glory.

She was stunned and heartbroken. But if she thought twice about allowing anger to play a part in her response, she never showed it. She met me with open arms of compassion I never could have expected, and she arranged for me to spend time with a nutritionist and counselor over the course of the next few months. Her love led me to slowly release the control-fueled resentments I held toward my dad, and her grace coaxed me into a place of slowly releasing the control-fueled relapses I'd wrestled with by myself. As I worked diligently to overcome my compulsions and addictions, she faithfully helped me to begin to navigate my new walk with Christ, subtly teaching me that the nutritionist and counselor could help, but if I desired true healing I had to set my own eyes on the Healer. Boldly helping me understand that an inherited faith wasn't a faith I could trust.

So with a gradually loosening grip on control and a determination for my college transition to turn a new page filled with hope, I limped into the first steps of my *own* walk with a King I still barely knew and made my way south to the wild Louisiana bayou.

# 5

## The Suicide of Simple

My parents and I rolled onto campus just in time for the start of spring semester in January 2008. Not only had I committed to play soccer at Louisiana State University, I had also worked to graduate high school a semester early and enroll in the spring instead of the usual fall start. I'm sure I seemed crazy, considering how physically grueling the off-season can be for a collegiate athlete, but I wanted to be present for an extra semester of fitness and training in the spring. Anything to get a leg up on the competition come fall. Choosing LSU hadn't been hard, but it had been one of those unexpected and inexplicable decisions I'd never thought I'd make.

The recruiting process while I was in high school had been competitive. Division I colleges from all across the nation had shown interest, sent letters, and invited me out for unofficial visits along the way. I was considered a top goalkeeper recruit for the Class of 2008—publications ranking me as one of the top six in the United States. To be honest, my ego loved the acknowledgment and the pursuit. The bigger the school, the bigger the program, the more I reveled in the letters I'd receive and the conversations I'd have with coaches. When I had to start really narrowing down my options, however, I first looked geographically. I knew I didn't want to go to the West Coast because I wanted my mom and dad to be able to come to my games. I knew I didn't want to go too far north either because there were few things I dreaded more than playing in the cold. So that left me juggling conferences and schools primarily in the southeast and, if you've been raised in the South, you know there are few things more storied and exciting than the SEC (in my opinion, at least).

Out of all the Southeastern Conference schools showing interest in me, LSU sat at the bottom of my list. They recruited more enthusiastically than any other school, with personalized letters arriving in my mailbox every single day of the week, but in my eyes, on the soccer side of things they were one of the least decorated programs in the league. I knew they had just acquired a new coaching staff a few years prior and were working passionately to build the program, but I wasn't convinced that the unfamiliar land of Louisiana was for me. In fact, my only perception of the swampy state had come several years prior when we took a family trip to New Orleans and I accidentally learned, at age ten, what a brothel was, and that apparently laws were a little different on this place called Bourbon Street. My poor parents. That was one vacation they probably wished we hadn't gotten quite as "whimsically lost in the city" like we tended to do when we traveled. There was so much eye-shielding and fast-paced walking that, eventually, my sister and I just stared at the ground and acted like we couldn't hear or see. I will say, though, that vacation introduced me to a hot, dark corner of Preservation Hall and some of the most intoxicating jazz music I'd ever heard. In considering LSU and the state of Louisiana, that muggy and magical memory always stood out to me.

The Tigers' persistence in recruiting paid off and my dad finally coaxed me into at least taking an unofficial visit to Baton Rouge. I reluctantly agreed and after an eight-hour trip we stepped out onto a campus that I couldn't believe. From its tall, looming oak trees to the red tile roofs and Spanish architecture–inspired buildings, it was mesmerizing. It was enchanting. The athletic facilities were unlike anything I'd ever seen and the rich history of the sports legacies written into the fields and stadiums were captivating. The coaches didn't need to say a word—LSU sold itself. Soccer may have been a less developed program there at the time, but I headed home to Georgia with a question posed to me: Did I want to join an already-storied program and be another average-sized fish in a big pond? Or did I want to rally behind a vision and belief, be a big fish in a small pond, and commit to helping grow a program's history?

Less than one week passed before I called up the coaches and verbally committed to play soccer for Louisiana State University.

## The First Few Steps of Faith

Just over one year later, on a cool January day in 2008, I hugged my mom and dad goodbye and stood alone at the starting gate of my biggest step of faith.

The college transition was in no way easy. Eager to explore all that my new home had to offer, I was often consumed by the excitement and intensity of change. I stumbled, as many young freshmen do, in finding my identity and learning the ins and outs of my new routine. The newfound freedom was disorienting. Figuring out who I wanted to be in college was equally confusing—especially crawling out of such a private identity crisis in high school.

Coming in a semester early, I didn't have a specific class to identify with, either. There were a lot of athletic advantages to arriving in the spring, but a big disadvantage was that I didn't have a built-in group of new teammates or classmates my age. At the start of a new school year, everyone understands new freshmen need to be oriented and given a chance to learn the ropes, but I landed smack in the middle of the school year and was a new kid on campus with no other new kids awkwardly navigating the transition alongside me. Most days it felt like drinking out of a fire hose—everything was intense and fast-paced. My suitemates were juniors, my teammates were all different ages and all over the place personality-wise, and my classmates were all well-adjusted to the study habits needed to survive college and the ins and outs of navigating their way around the university. As for me, I was none of those things. Everything was new—and seemingly worth trying.

For a while I really struggled socially and behaviorally—and, often times, just plain sensibly. Once again, I didn't concretely know who I was or who I was supposed to be. I was impressionable and gullible, willing to try whatever the group I was hanging out with was doing. Experimenting with alcohol was new to me, the freedoms of living on my own blindsided me, and the longing to find my niche once again pulled at my puppet strings. But while I may have stumbled and struggled to find my groove in some areas, there were a few avenues I channeled my discipline and focus toward in which I excelled tremendously. Regarding athletics, nothing could distract me.

Athletically and physically, that spring was a time of adjustment and intentionality. Isaiah 40:29 reads, "He gives strength to the weary and increases the power of the weak." God very quickly began to empower me in my weakness as I crawled out of my disordered eating habits and control issues and wholeheartedly focused on surrendering my compulsive needs for control to Him. Through the incredible structure of the LSU soccer program and the amazing provisions of the university, I found my focus reinspired. By giving God control, I was able to not only gradually strengthen my faith and dependence but to physically strengthen my body as well—in a healthy manner. I worked, relentlessly, taking no shortcuts in my healing and development, and channeled my energy into learning how to adjust my skillset to compete effectively at the collegiate level. I knew I had been recruited to hopefully become a first-string starter as a freshman, so I made it my goal to earn my stripes and prove my worth right out of the gate in our spring scrimmages. And by holding shutouts against both national powerhouses UNC and Duke, I felt like I did just that. After remaining at school through the summer and finding my second home in the weight room, come fall I felt well-equipped to step onto the field and help lead my team.

Though fresh in my independent faith walk, I felt fairly well-equipped there too. The lies and twisted thoughts hadn't fully subsided, but with each step I drew nearer to Christ, it became clearer how to identify those deceitful thoughts and draw them out. Satan constantly tried to penetrate my mind and heart from new and creative angles, but the blessings and provisions surrounding me at LSU helped me muffle his lies.

One of the enemy's boldest attempts to twist my thoughts came disguised in a surprising way, but one I've learned is far more common than I realized at the time. It's a plague, really. A contagious lie so many of us believe or have wrestled with throughout our walk. A subtle manipulation of thought causing hordes of believers to stay silent—content with an unseen, unheard walk.

*This faith walk is fine. In fact, it's good.*

*You can call yourself a Christian. There's nothing wrong with that. In fact, it's a popular title to have. There are churches all around. You're in the Bible Belt, after all. So this is normal.*

*But you need to be careful.*

*It would be best for you to keep this newfound faith to yourself.*

*You know perfectly well you don't understand it all, and your behavior and choices sometimes sing a different tune.*

*If you're going to be outspoken about God, about His Word, then you need to know all of the answers. You need to be living perfectly first.*

*You need to be able to quote Scripture. You need to know the chronology of it all. If you don't know all of the Scriptures and fully comprehend grace and have a response for anyone who tries to throw it back in your face, then you lose.*

*You need to have an answer for anyone who opposes you or asks questions. You need to be able to lead other people to the faith. If you can't defend the faith properly, then you're going to look like a fool.*

*If you can't effectively share the gospel or preach your testimony then you're nowhere near ready to be bold. You won't be good enough. A good enough Christian, at least.*

*So be a Christian. That's fine.*

*But shh . . . keep it to yourself. You don't have to be one of the bold ones. Don't get uncomfortable.*

*Just blend.*

*Shh . . . Keep living as you are and you'll be fine.*

Those words almost won. Those thoughts and my nervousness and my comfort level almost rationalized truth into those lies. As if God's grace was ordinary enough to silently coast through a room unnoticed—to coast through my life unseen and unheard. As if this strength I could feel Him rebuilding and this hope I felt Him restoring and these blessings I saw Him ordaining were average enough for me to keep quiet.

No. With each new step of faith, new words were finding their place in my heart and on my lips, and when the enemy attacked I'd nervously fight back.

So whether you eat or drink or whatever you do, do it all for the glory of God. (1 Cor. 10:31)

But I trust in your unfailing love;
  my heart rejoices in your salvation.
I will sing the Lord's praise,
  for he has been good to me. (Ps. 13:5–6)

My tongue will proclaim your righteousness,
  your praises all day long. (Ps. 35:28)

As for me, I would give God praise. Even when I was Googling verses and fumbling through the Word and close to completely unaware of any of the context of what I was reading, God's truth still found me and constantly reminded me that He wasn't asking me to be perfect. He wasn't asking me to have all the answers or to know all the Scriptures or to be the "best Christian" before I openly shared my faith. He wasn't asking me to have it all figured out—rather He was gently reminding me I had nothing figured out. And lovingly teaching me that, even still, He would meet all my needs.

God coaxed me into such a place of peace with each passing day that I found my way to my knees. Through imperfect prayer and clueless Bible searching, He still met me. He welcomed me. He reminded me that, in time, He would teach me and grow me. But what He desired first, in my brand-new walk of faith, was simply to step out and give Him the glory. Not to be shy. Not to be afraid. But in all things, in everything, to start by giving Him praise.

So I set my mind to doing just that. In all things I worked to give God the glory. In response to my small steps of faithfulness, I began to notice even more beautiful and unquestionable blessings. For one, my relationship with my dad drastically improved. I knew he was sad having his baby girl so far away, but I never expected our friendship to mend so tightly. We chatted on the phone throughout the day, with nine or ten calls back and forth becoming nothing out of the ordinary. As a former college football player who saw his dreams and goals cut short by injury, he delighted in my collegiate journey.

My academics excelled as well as I found a rhythm in balancing soccer and my studies. My behavior leveled out as the luster of "new" wore off so many tempting, empty things and I started to discover who I was as a young, independent woman and find my own groove as a college athlete. My confidence and excitement when I stepped into my first official season as a Tiger felt unparalleled to anything I'd ever felt before. Little did I know the blessing God was about to orchestrate through the sport I loved was unparalleled to anything the soccer world had ever seen.

## My Ninety-Yard Blessing

It was my second game ever as a freshman in college and early in the second half of a home game against BYU. I didn't think much of it when a foul was called just outside my goalkeeper's box. I waved off my defender and strolled up to the ball, scanning the field for an open player and figuring out where I wanted to place it. I suppose nobody thought much of me jogging up about thirty yards from the end line to take the free kick. After all, I hadn't just been recruited for my shot-saving ability between the pipes; it was already widely known that my leg was a weapon for our team's attack.

I spotted one of our fastest forwards pressing hard on BYU's back line and set my mind to playing the ball over the cluster of players around midfield in order to give her a shot at turning a quick attack. With that, I lined up, paced my strides, and let the rhythm of my technique flow through me. A few soft steps and I kicked the ball.

I knew the moment I made contact that it was a solid kick. An experienced player can hear the difference. You can feel it. And that kick felt *good*. What I didn't realize was just how far the strike was soaring on that still August night. I glanced down to backpedal back to my net, but the screams of the crowd quickly forced me to look up.

One bounce was all it took. BYU's goalkeeper had cheated off her line to cut the angle on our speeding forward. But in doing so she completely misjudged the ball's drop. In fact, *no one* could have judged the ball's drop. Because it didn't drop—for seventy yards. By the time it hit the ground it was too late for her to adjust. All it took was a single bounce, and I watched as the keeper leapt up and arched back as the ball curled over

71

her outstretched arms. Bounce . . . bounce . . . and into the net it rolled.

I had just scored a ninety-yard goal.

The stands erupted. My teammates came sprinting. It felt, in that moment, like the whole earth was shaking. The fans shook the stadium with cheers and applause and the announcer's voice boomed over the loud speaker. I yelled in shock as my teammates piled around me and the celebration lasted for what felt like a century. I don't think it clicked in that moment that somehow I had just achieved a feat in the sport that had never been documented before. A feat that I most certainly couldn't have accomplished through my own strength and power. A feat God would use to begin building a platform bigger than I could have fathomed.

In that moment all that I wanted to do was look up. My daddy was sitting right beneath the press box and even in the midst of all the chaos and noise, I knew I heard his voice in the stands. It was a voice yelling with the echoes of a pride born so deep within his heart it couldn't be imitated—only felt. A pride and excitement so organic, so true, that I felt its vibrations down to my core. My dad was yelling so loudly I thought he was going to burst. He already looked, at any given moment, like he was about forty-five months pregnant, so with the screaming added on top of his overwhelming frame, he looked like Fat Tarzan pounding his chest up there. Catching his eye, I saw a smile strung wider than any I had ever seen before. I swear his teeth were touching his ears. I saw a joy beaming so fantastically from him he took on a glow, and I'm still surprised he didn't rip his shirt off.

As the game continued and the play progressed, that man was still screaming. Still cheering so loudly I doubted the people in the press box could even hear themselves think. Ten minutes later . . . still cheering. Oozing with a passion that seemed to have just been waiting to overflow. A passion that a man, usually so disciplined and stoic in his demeanor, usually able to wrestle down such deep-rooted struggles, couldn't control. A passion, I would later learn, I was fortunate to witness. In that moment I didn't want to let it go.

The next thing I knew that goal was splashed across the television, magazines, and the internet. Appearing as a #3 play on SportsCenter Top 10 plays—an extreme rarity for women's college soccer—that incredible kick was suddenly being watched and rewatched all around the globe. Strewn across the pages of *Sports Illustrated* and linked onto YouTube, Break.com, and countless other sites, the energy of that play took on a life of its own. LSU Soccer was put on the map in a matter of moments, and recognition and attention seemed to come to our team effortlessly.

Throughout the rest of that season, my daddy was always there. A relationship blossomed between me and him that was so beautiful and pure I felt humbled to be a part of it. The season was record-breaking. In continuing to work my hardest athletically and, in all the ways I knew how, giving God the glory, I felt the blessings continue to rain down. By the end of my fall semester I was on top of the world. I had played every minute in goal for the Tigers in 2008 and helped lead our top-ranked defensive unit to the most dominant stats in the SEC. I broke single-season records at LSU and became a conference contender in the net. I was named Freshman All-American, Louisiana Freshman of the Year, and a member of the SEC All-Freshman Team, along with numerous other awards. I was invincible. Untouchable. At that point, you couldn't have convinced me life would ever be anything less than all I dreamed.

That was until I returned to Georgia for Christmas break and, on January 2, 2009, my daddy didn't come home.

## Missing

It was interesting how quickly my spiritual perspective had shifted. Returning to Georgia for Christmas, I was riding high from the successes of the season. While I wasn't still stuck in the misconstrued maze of the cultural Christianity I'd always settled for at home, the whirlwind of my new faith walk and the successes of my freshman year had left me with a different, yet still incomplete, perspective of God. In my mind, being a Christian meant giving the glory to God and benefitting, in response, from His immeasurable blessings. I felt naive for seemingly missing the point for so long. I was convinced that a walk with the Lord guaranteed provision and blessing and success and ease. After all, that was the model I had seen play out for the past year in my own life. I had no reason to believe that God's economy of value didn't work exactly like that.

I was happy to be surrounded by the nostalgia of home and was blissfully unaware of any changes or tensions that existed outside of my own bubble. I remember my dad calling me into his room a few days after I had returned home. As I sat on the edge of the bed, I noticed a hint of fatigue in his eyes. A dimming of the twinkle that was so familiar—the twinkle I had seen shining by that soccer field just a few months before. But a fresh glimmer quickly sparked in his excitement to show me the reason he had called me in to the room, so I didn't think much of the sadness I thought I'd briefly seen. On his bedside table radio, he played the broadcast that was recorded during

74

my ninety-yard goal and beamed with joy. For what must have been ten straight minutes, we laughed together, replayed the sound clip, and bounced on his bed, drunk with pride and excitement. I'll never forget the joy of that moment—nor will I forget the single tear I saw him wipe from his cheek when he thought I wasn't looking.

In the days that followed, life was every bit as normal as it had been in my youth. Our family exchanged stories, visited friends, and shared laughs. That Christmas was just like every other Isom family Christmas: dramatic, chaotic, dizzying. But comfortable. Throughout that time, my dad began opening up to me about deep, personal things we had never discussed before. Thoughts of his childhood, details of his relationships.

Looking back, I see now that he was different. He made himself so vulnerable yet so inaccessible at the same time. I knew he'd had a hard time adjusting to both of his girls being out of the house and off at school, but he seemed weakened, distracted by something, and tired. I attributed our newfound vulnerability to circumstance. We had missed each other, I was growing up, he was growing older, and we were both growing closer. I savored those moments, deeply.

New Year's came and went in a matter of four riveting quarters. My family created fantastic memories at the Peach Bowl, where LSU pommelled Georgia Tech in the Georgia Dome. With unbelievable seats and friends in town to entertain, I was oblivious to the drastic shift in emotions that had taken place in our family that day. I recognized that my mom seemed out of character—discontent, frustrated, resentful. But the energy of the evening prevented me from asking questions. I dismissed the situation and figured it was none of my business. My distracted and idealistic rationale convinced me that God would care for our family. Whatever the problem was, God would sort it out. I was giving Him the glory so He would, in turn, glorify us. That's how it worked, right?

January 2 was the day that everything came to a crashing halt. I remember, so vividly, standing in the boutique at my winter job that morning when my cell phone rang. My dad and I talked on the phone way too often every day, so when I looked at the caller ID and saw his name, I couldn't help but smile. He knew I was at work, he knew I couldn't talk. But best friends have no problem breaking the rules. Our conversation was every bit as normal as usual. He asked me how my day was going, what I was up to at work, when I would be home. We made small talk for about ten minutes until a wave of customers came in and I finally convinced him that I had to go.

Before hanging up I casually said, "Love ya!" and lowered the phone. But this time I heard his voice call out on the other end of the line. I lifted the receiver back to my ear and heard what seemed like the voice of a different man. In a tone so eerily calm, so genuine, and so sad, my daddy simply said, "I love you so much, Morlan."

I stood for a moment, curious and unsettled, then replied in as stoic and truthful a tone as he, "I love you too, Dad. More than anything."

*Click.*

I returned home from work that evening around six o'clock and made my way inside, strolling past the vacant space where my dad's truck was usually parked. I remember finding it odd that he wasn't home yet, especially considering the fact that, a family man through and through, he never seemed to get home later than 5:30. But I brushed off my concern and made my way up the back porch steps. When I walked inside, there was an energy and tension in the house that is still difficult to describe. The air seemed tight and still. But I was wrapped up in my own thoughts and to-dos and didn't think too much of the quiet chill.

Over the next few hours, my sister made her way in and out of my room. Sloan seemed disheveled and concerned, asking me over and over where Dad was and if I had spoken to him. I laughed off her worry and assured her he was fine, but her angst seemed to build as the minutes ticked by. I tried calling him a number of times, but after thirty minutes of his phone going straight to voicemail, my anxiety began to rise as well. Just as I was going to make my way downstairs to talk to my mom, her voice echoed up the steps. A voice shaken with fear—one that demanded attention. A voice unfamiliar from a woman so steady and strong. She called us into the formal living room and we came down to find her feverishly pacing, her quick steps mirroring the quickening pace of our hearts.

My mom's cheeks were ruddy and hot, yet her demeanor was so forcefully calm that she took on the mannerisms of a marionette. I could see that she wanted to erupt, to cry out in fear, to panic and scream. But being the woman of poise and faith that she was, she remained as calm and steadfast as she could, undoubtedly held together by the grace of God alone. She proceeded to tell us of the events that had passed in the last two days. Of financial issues and complete confusion and phone calls with the IRS and unpaid taxes and overwhelming deception. She had unknowingly uncovered a series of lies my dad had been concealing, and now that the truth had come to the surface he was nowhere to be found.

With no time to explain in more detail, she told us that she had been trying to call my dad all evening. She took us back to her room and showed us a simple, handwritten note he had left beneath the phone. A note that simply read, "I do love you," and had his name signed beneath it. Mind racing, heart pounding, I found my body tensing and my nerves coiling tight. I couldn't put the pieces together. I couldn't wrap my head around the situation. There was so little detail, so little explanation. What was going on? Where was my dad? Were my parents going to go to jail? How big was this lie? How were we going to get in touch with him? When was he coming home?

It was then that I noticed a blinking light on the voicemail machine by the phone and asked my mom who had called. Reluctantly, she told Sloan and me that she had found a voice message along with the note. She pressed the button and I immediately heard my father's voice. In that moment the reality and severity of the situation hit me—the instant I heard him speak. Because I knew it was my father talking on the answering machine, but it wasn't my *daddy's* voice. It was hollow and broken and empty. It was a voice so desperate, so shattered, that it sounded like a stranger. He sounded like it was taking every ounce of his energy and pride to muster a noise, draining his heart with every word.

He apologized. Said he needed to drive around and clear his head. Said he needed to be alone for a while to figure things out. Said he loved us and would always love us. And said little else before he said goodbye.

That was when true fear set in. Where was my dad and how were we going to find him? My mom, sister, and I sat up for hours trying to put the pieces together, giving accounts of our day and the last time we had seen him or talked to him, calling friends and family—anyone who may know where he was, anyone who may be able to contact him. With each lost lead, a hot burn slid down my spine as we tried, in desperation, to find him. I could feel the enemy feeding off of our fear and I knew my faith and trust were fading faster than I wanted to believe.

When exhaustion set in, Sloan and I lay down on our mom's bed. I squeezed my daddy's pillow tight and sucked in his aroma as deeply as my lungs could muster. While my mom sat up in the kitchen making countless calls and desperately seeking help, my sister and I cried ourselves to sleep. Holding each other tight, we offered empty assurances to ease one another's angst and hoped that everything would just disappear. That my dad would come driving up and everything would go back to normal. That some resolution would come soon and that we'd be able to cuddle up next to our daddy in this very same spot the next night.

That was the first night I couldn't pray. I was too confused and too blindsided to even think of what to say. I couldn't muster the strength to reach out to a God who seemed nowhere near. And that hot burn that had coiled around my spine seemed to linger in the depths of me. Maybe you've wrestled with the same struggle at some point—unsure of what's even sufficient, what words could possibly wrap around a situation that feels bigger than any words. That feels bigger than our own strength. It wasn't that I didn't desire to reach out to God, I simply didn't have the words. In the midst of so much confusion, my heart just couldn't find its way.

At some point in the night I stumbled up to my own bedroom, but no more than a few hours into our shallow rest, my sister and I were woken by a scream. I could hear my mom's feet sprinting up the basement steps from our home office and a sheet of paper crackling in her hand.

"Get in the car! Now! Get in the car!"

My sister came bounding up the steps to grab me, and after I threw on my shoes and a jacket we fearfully ran downstairs. My mom, grabbing boxes of papers, contact information, her purse, and her shoes, ordered Sloan and me into my sister's Mustang GT. As we sped around town searching for any place my dad might be, I remembered the sheet of paper my mom had been holding and I begged to see what she'd seen.

It took a while for my frantic, frazzled mom to concede, but in desperation she finally shoved the crumpled sheet of paper into the backseat.

"Fine, read it. Then help me! Please!"

Absentmindedly smoothing out the creases in the paper, I looked down and read. Horror overcame me. It didn't take long to realize the sheet I was holding was an email she'd found from my daddy. A suicide email, addressed to our family.

It's hard to understand how someone could sum up their life on three-quarters of a page of paper. But my dad's suicide letter did just that. It was vague and empty and shallow. As my mom sped through town, stopping at every location she could imagine my dad might be, my sister made desperate phone calls to the police, my dad's friends, his coworkers, and family members. But with life moving five hundred miles per hour around me, I found myself frozen. The world surrounding me seemed to turn to molasses, slowly flowing by in a foggy, glazed state. I couldn't peel my eyes from the letter in my hands.

He first apologized. He explained, in complete brevity, that he couldn't overcome his own personal demons. He referred to himself as a lone soul and he offered his guidance for how we could move forward without him. Then he wrote a small paragraph to my mom, followed by a brief paragraph about my sister. And lastly, a short series of sentences about me. His words were generic and gross—stripped of any sincerity or passion. As if he were a shell, void of emotion, when he wrote them. As if he had already accepted his fate and telling us his plans was just a formality.

When I snapped back into reality, we were pulling up to his office building and all I could see were police lights and uniformed officials. My mom had tried calling the police the night before when my dad didn't come home, but seeing as how he had only been gone a few hours, there wasn't much they could do. Apparently later in the night she had thought to call the suicide hotline to simply pick their brains on if they thought the specific circumstances warranted concern. Their reaction and instruction led to the involvement of the police. And early the next morning, on January 3, my mom discovered the email. It wasn't long until we stood in a parking lot surrounded by flashing lights and concerned faces and an air of desperation that made everything far too *real*. My dad was a known attorney in town, so the faces of the officers who surrounded us weren't unattached strangers just doing their jobs—they were colleagues and peers and badges who knew and loved Big John.

Upon my mom's instruction, we ran straight into his office, hysterically searching for any shred of evidence that might provide a clue to his whereabouts—frantically trying to find my daddy before my daddy gave up. I'd like to write that I was in any way helpful. But the fact of the matter is I felt numb. I sat at his desk and stared at his blank computer and shuffled through mounds of paper as if I knew what I was looking for. We were in a race against time and the seconds seemed to be ticking by faster and faster, but my muscles and my mind just couldn't keep up. The police filled the office building, fielding calls and tracing clues. There was so much noise—so much commotion. Phones ringing, people yelling, papers shuffling. Chaos and voices and sound. Then before I knew it—nothing. Silence fell all around.

I'll never forget the moment when everything stopped. My mom, my sister, and I were all behind my dad's desk. But suddenly the air hung thick with unspoken words. The three of us looked up at the same time and saw three officers in the doorway. The looks on their faces were indescribable. My mom stumbled back and demanded they walk away, get back to work, and keep searching for her husband. But the officers didn't move until, finally, one spoke up.

"Ma'am, we have found your husband."

A flicker of hope! A relief, oh what a sweet relief! A moment of utter joy, a moment of—

"I'm sorry, let us clarify: we've found your husband's remains."

It was then that my world froze. No child should ever have to endure the sound of their mother's heart breaking. The sight of their sister shattering and falling broken to the floor. The sound that I realized was resonating from the deepest depths of me wasn't a cry or a scream. It was a sound of utter anguish. It poured from me with such ferocity I could feel the heat rise from my soul. I felt a numbness overwhelm my body and expand into every crevice of my being. In that instant, our perfect family was shattered. Our perfect lives were destroyed. Normal was an illusion. All I could do was heave.

My dad's delicately built world had crumbled around him in a matter of days. The secret my mom had stumbled upon was a lie woven through fourteen years of life's tapestry. It was all so avoidable. There was no infidelity, no impurity—but there was deceit. My dad had allowed his personal issues he protected so privately to escalate. I think that by avoiding handling the "tough stuff" of life on a day-to-day basis and instead allowing it to accumulate through time, he lost his way. Financial issues mounted. Disorganization snowballed. Shame grew. His struggle to independently handle the things he believed were his duty and responsibility, as a man, seemed to challenge his identity as a husband and a father and a provider. His pride and his desire to maintain a carefully crafted perception left him overwhelmed, overstimulated, and struggling in a hole of insurmountable depth.

There is much to be said about a humble country boy who builds himself into a man of earthly prestige and success. My mom once told me that sometimes, those who come from such humble beginnings carry their pride in their back pocket along with their crisp hundred-dollar bills. While there is much to be respected and admired in men who have the strength to build their own empires, the foundations of their intentions must be pure. Never forgetting who they serve and what is required of them. Never sacrificing integrity for the sake of image— particularly when they have everything to lose.

I don't think my father had the capacity to handle the fact that his pride and issues had damaged the one thing he cherished above all else: his family. I don't think he could face me and my sister with the truth, nor do I think he could face his mother or his wife. Unwilling to reach out for help and blindsided as his great weaknesses were brought into the light, he panicked. The personal demons he already wrestled with in so many ways seemed to have a stranglehold on a man who, at his core, yearned for the simplicity of boyhood. In the face of his greatest fears those personal demons coaxed him to a place of desperation.

He had run. He had picked up in the middle of the day and made his way back toward his humble roots. Back toward his childhood home in Alabama. He took every precaution to assure his success. He came home to get his guns in the middle of the day, leaving the note and the message when nobody was around to stop him. He turned off his phone and severed any chance of contact. Then he drove. Away from his problems, away from his responsibilities.

I'd like to think something snapped in my dad's mind. I'd like to think his actions were rash and his decisions were spontaneous. But the fact of the matter is that my dad spent a great deal of time thinking that day. From the time he left his office at lunch to the time his suicide email was sent in the early morning hours, he had spent hours drowning in thought. Hours harboring a war within his spirit. Hours hosting a battle in his soul. I won't write much more about what I don't know. It hurts too badly to let my imagination wander. But I do know one thing: my dad was a beautiful man. He was also a man riddled with wreckage and personal sin-struggles, paralyzed by fear and caught in Satan's snares. A man who loved others far more than he was ever capable of loving himself. And *that* is what breaks my heart the most.

The police were finally able to track him down only because one call had been made from his cell phone in that time. One single call, to 911. He had distanced himself far enough from his family but close enough to his home. He had checked into a hotel room, neatly hung up his clothes, written on a small slip of paper what he wished to be done with his body and called 911. I can only assume he did this so that a maid wouldn't walk in on the scene and be scarred by a pain she had no need to feel. My daddy then sat down on the hotel bed with a gun and gave up.

It was before dawn on January 3, 2009 that my daddy put a gun to his heart and pulled the trigger.

And it was January 3, 2009 that I took off running from God.

84

# 6

## Dr. Jekyll and Mr. Hyde

I lost myself in 2009.

The funeral home preparation room smelled like formaldehyde and wreckage. The worst kind of wreckage. The kind that ravaged and tore at me as I stood by the cold metal table and stared at the white sheet outlining my dad's body.

I wasn't surprised when no tears could come as they pulled back the sheet and I saw his pale face. There were none left to shed. Not after the past few days of relentless crying. Every ounce of me felt dry as I stood over his body and rubbed my fingers over the small hole in his chest, just above his once beating heart. In that moment my heart felt just as dead as the broken one left in his body. I struggled to wrap my mind around how such a small hole had taken down such a giant. How that familiar chest and those strong, broad shoulders, and those coarse, loving hands could sag so heavy and lifeless.

It was all so unexceptional. So unimpressive. So final. I imagined he preferred it that way. To go out as unceremoniously as he felt he deserved. To exit just as he believed he had walked through life—unremarkably. Because that's how it all felt. *Suicide*. Dramatic and horrific and theatrical, yes, but more than anything—unremarkable. Because in the end, it was just that—the *end*. Nothing anyone could do could change that.

Or maybe he felt heroic in some twisted, broken way. His suicide letter had mentioned that his decision would be for our benefit—he would be sparing us the problems he always felt he was creating. He explained he was wrestling demons, so maybe he thought ending the torment would finally set him free. Maybe he thought the insurance money would do something to bandage the wounds he left our family.

Either way, his twisted perspective and wrecked mentality and deceit-fueled demons were the same demons quickly overcoming me. It was with the thought of that blood-soaked hotel bed and the echo of that pistol shot to the chest that I took off running.

And running.

As far and as fast as my mangled heart would carry me.

## Questioning God

It's amazing how quickly our hearts can move from praising God to blaming Him when life's circumstances suddenly become overwhelming. It's as if, at times, our threshold for pain has the strongest pull on our loyalty. As if we're willing to walk in faith until true faith is actually required of us in great quantity. As if the degree of affliction we face in our lives is somehow directly related to the degree of God's capability. Pain-induced arrogance. It's our greatest defense mechanism. And one that always sends us running.

I first ran into denial. Denial of my circumstances and denial of my new reality. This couldn't be *my* life. This couldn't be *my* story. None of this numbness, this pain, this wreckage—none of this was in the plan. It was all too overwhelming.

I can't tell you the number of times I caught myself trying to call my daddy. The subconscious habits were the most painful to break. Every time I'd be reminded the line was disconnected. Every time I'd feel the stabbing reminder that things weren't ever going to be the same. Every time I'd be forced to remember I was never going to hear my dad's voice again.

I had to return to LSU just a few weeks after I stood next to my dad's casket and hugged the hundreds of friends and family members who filed through the sanctuary. Every face mirrored the one before it—dumbfounded by the incomprehensible truth. Soaked in shock that this piercing pain had so quickly entered their stories too. A part of me wanted to stay home and help my stunned mom and stoic sister pick up the pieces of our family's shattered story. But another part of me longed to run away from everything—the sounds, the smells, the memories, the triggers. To get far away from the constant reminders that my brain refused to believe were true. It didn't take much convincing for me to pack up and head back to school. I needed to continue my education. I needed to lace up my cleats and continue competing. After all, my mom assured me, it's what my dad would have wanted me to do.

When the staff had recruited me to LSU they had made many promises about the quality of care and provision at the school. I should have known their words were true when my coaches and teammates traveled from around the country to stand alongside me at my dad's funeral. But if there was any doubt left in my mind, it was dispelled as soon as I stepped back onto campus and realized everything they had set up for me to help me grieve and process moving forward at school. From a grief counselor to an academic support staff, it seemed like every administrator on campus was made aware of my circumstances and prepared to help support me through my healing. Even the coaches informed me I was free to miss any spring practices I needed to as I healed. I missed one. And the next day I stayed after practice to make up for my absence, running sprints on my own.

I wanted to focus. And I wanted to remain disciplined. Part of my heart wanted to receive all of the warmth that was offered to me; part of me was still that innocent girl watching her proud daddy cheering in the stands. This part of me yearned for normalcy and purity. So for a while I worked to cling to happy memories: childhood lake trips on our wave runner, Saturday afternoons watching football in our pajamas, the look on his face after I'd scored that goal. I fought for joy for a stretch of time, but it was hard to hold a smile when my mind constantly crawled back to envisioning his face in the hotel room, envisioning his body on that bed, wondering what he could have been thinking and feeling. And growing angrier that now he was nothing more than *dead*.

Like an old familiar friend, the enemy capitalized on my emotional depression and was never far from me. It wasn't long before my heart shifted to anger. And resentment. And hatred toward my dad as the initial shock began to wear off and the unyielding pain started to seep through. A pain so debilitating, so crippling, it made it hard to even think. I began to foster feelings I had never truly known before. Feelings of passionate resentment. Feelings of confusion, jealousy, pain. Feelings of envy, impatience, obsession. Feelings of loneliness, deep inadequacy, weakness. Feelings of fear, crippling fear. Feelings

88

of abandonment—not only abandonment from my father but abandonment from God. How could my dad have done this to our family? How could God not have stopped the situation from happening?

What happened to giving God the glory and the blessings raining down? What happened to the mountaintop? To giving praise and, in turn, receiving protection? To glorifying God and, in response, finding His favor? This wasn't what my life was supposed to look like. This wasn't how it was supposed to all play out. This couldn't come from a *good* God. Because if God was good, if He was holy, how could He let this disaster happen? I knew no hope, I knew no joy, I knew no happily ever after.

I ran, next, from hope. From any trust in God's truth.

A good God?

A loving God?

I didn't know if I believed *that* God was true.

I felt a hole so deep and so painful in my heart that it burned in my chest. I felt numb to any kindness or compassion shown to me, convinced that absolutely nobody knew what I was feeling. Convinced that nobody could relate to my situation or totally grasp how wrecked my world was. The further I ran, the more I found myself convinced that I would never know normal again. While I had people all around me constantly reminding me of God's goodness and His sovereignty, I felt nothing. Nothing but pain and anguish and suffering. Every mention of a God who loved me only left me more resentful of the God who I felt had left me—who seemed nowhere to be found in my time of need.

Because in my mind, I didn't feel God. I didn't feel anything outside of confusion and suffering. If I couldn't feel God then I didn't want God—this God whom I believed had left me scorned and wandering.

## The Masks We Hide Behind

Next I ran into depression and anxiety. It was hard for me to grasp how I could be so wrapped in love and surrounded by support yet still feel so unbelievably alone. I guess I understood how my father had felt.

My grief manifested itself physically. Rashes formed and hair fell out and skin peeled off in sheets. One week I would have a cold, and the next strep throat. The next week it would be pinkeye or some other inexplicable condition brought on by the stress on my anxious heart. Noise increasingly began to irritate me. People talking, music blaring, the sound of crunching or smacking or eating. It was all too much—the noises were overwhelming. I'd find myself in a fit of rage—with my blood pressure spiking and sudden difficulty breathing and my skin becoming hot and flushed—whenever sound agitated me. I needed silence. I needed space to think. To process. To breathe.

But I never felt like there was time. There was no escaping reality. The world was continuing to turn and people were moving on. I felt, oftentimes, like I was supposed to be further along in processing everything than my numb and aching heart allowed me to be. I was on autopilot. Unable to work through so many emotions as quickly as society seemingly demanded. I felt guilty for how long it was taking me to wrap my head around everything. In many ways, I felt like everyone was starting to move forward without me, and if I didn't compensate somehow then I'd inevitably become forgotten or go unseen.

It didn't take long for me to realize that if I was going to keep up with my carefully built world and maintain my well-crafted appearance of poise and strength, I was going to have to take up the art of acting. We should all win Academy Awards, really.

For how skilled we are at faking "fine." For how talented we are at hiding our pain in order to play the game. Like so many of us do when our pain is greater than our purpose, I quickly adopted a "fake-it-till-you-make-it" mentality.

The masks we hide behind are well crafted, aren't they? They're intricate and detailed and comforting. Are you wearing one right now? We're chameleons of identity—our masks hide our weaknesses and our vulnerable places and our scars. Maybe we find it freeing to know we can be anyone we want to be. The problem is that behind the masks we can't ever actually be who we were created to be. In fact, we can't ever even *be*. Not when we're always hiding.

In the public eye and to my family, I was strong. A woman of character and grace. I found it easier to wear my mask and pretend like I was healing. It seemed like I was thriving in my lifeless, vacant walk of faith. I forced smiles, gave memorized praises to the King I publicly claimed, and spoke of the Word of God to anyone who asked how my heart was recovering. I crawled through my hidden wreckage talking the talk, but most days my heart bled bankrupt, numb and unwilling to walk the walk.

Behind closed doors and in my spirit, I was dark. I was self-absorbed in my own grief and increasingly desperate for that gaping hole in my heart to be filled. I was a lost little girl. With powerful spiritual warfare ripping me at my seams, I started living recklessly, leaving a trail of destruction behind me. Inside, my depression owned me. Desperation consumed me. Pain so deeply overwhelmed me that I became willing to compromise anything for some relief.

Each sin seemed so tempting. Any pleasure a moment could offer seemed so appealing. Even if it was temporary—it was an escape. Escape was all I ever looked for when I was running. The hole in my heart was gaping and all I wanted was to fill the emptiness inside of me—with anything.

So I ran from my inhibitions. From my discernment, my principles.

That's the next place my constant running steered me.

There was so much I could get away with in the darkness. I had dabbled in college temptations early in my freshman year, so finding my way back to those things was easy. The partying and the drinking—they were great distractions. They invited me in and convinced me I was accepted and welcomed me into an escape where, even if just for a night, I wouldn't have to remember or hurt or feel anything. I indulged in all that lifestyle had to offer. It was easy to be adopted into. In fact, giving in to that scene felt rewarding. And accepting. And *good* to me.

The truth of the matter is that my running led me right into the thick of all that those around me seemed to care about and revel in and enjoy. In the midst of the masses nobody could see I was hurting because my depressed indulgences perfectly disguised me as "just another college kid." I looked average. I blended—for once, I just blended. So the alcohol flowed and every ounce of me relished the sins that distracted others from my scars that I was sure still showed.

I wonder how many others around me were in my same boat, trying to fill a God-sized hole with sin-sized pieces and simply "blending" with the brokenness of the masses in the meantime. I wonder how many were hurting. I wonder if anyone knew I was in pain. But then again, that's the problem with the masks we hide behind—they work well. Too well. We're rarely aware of the cries for help that are masked in the sin-filled "good times."

But it was never enough. The hole in my heart just couldn't be filled. The temporary pleasures always faded and the next morning's hangover was always escorted by the emotional pain of what was real. You'd think that realizing numbing the wounds would never actually help them for longer than just a little while would have been enough to help me snap into reality and handle my pain appropriately and move forward in hope. But, for whatever reason, the pieces struggled to click into place. I never seemed to learn from what I'd been told. My curiosity just had to hold the experience. I found new ways to keep numbing my pain and I rationalized logic away as my wrecked and foolish heart continued to indulge.

Eventually, when my lips found their way around a bottle every weekend, my body began to find its way to any other temporary pleasure it could find. In desperate need for some temporary high, I found myself struggling more and more with pornography, masturbation, and promiscuity that I rationalized as normal and fine.

My mind rationalized that I was still technically a virgin, and as long as I didn't go all the way then there was no harm in pushing the envelope. It was all so easy, so accessible. Even when I woke up nauseous and half-naked the next morning, my mind would rationalize that the gaping hole in my heart had been filled for a night. In my desperation, I'd sometimes convince myself that was enough. I rationalized it was my body and they were my choices and I could do what I wanted. I gave pieces of myself to any boy who could satiate my desire to temporarily feel loved. I recklessly pursued empty relationships and misguided lust. I gave and gave and gave. And in return, I was left even emptier and void of trust.

I was a modern-day Dr. Jekyll and Mr. Hyde, polished and poised on the surface but with everything to hide.

My sophomore soccer season wasn't easy—unfamiliar, even, without my dad in the stands. Somehow I broke records, yet again, and helped anchor a defensive unit that was unrivaled in the SEC. I helped my team win an SEC West Championship, and place second overall in the conference. But the truth was that the energy I mustered on game day was about all the energy there was in me. I was exhausted, worn thin from a year of searching for sin-sized pieces to fill the God-sized hole within me.

It had been a year of running. At the breaking point of each broken day, I understood why my dad did what he did. Even amid the highs of a dominant season, at times I saw it as a viable option. Suicide. How easy it would have been to end it all. It was tempting, at times, to give in to the rationale of genetics—as much as I resembled my mom, I was my father's daughter. If he was capable of such a bold act, maybe I was capable of it too. Bound for it, even.

I was shattered. I could feel the tightening grip of Satan's cold fingers and the sting of his hot breath down my spine. He was gaining power, gaining strength from my emotional vulnerability. Sucking my innocence, my ambition, my light from me. Capitalizing on my weakness and catering to my darkest emotions. Reveling in my running. I didn't even try to fight.

While the fall semester of soccer had been fine, I was aching and exhausted and dying to get home to my mom and my sister for Thanksgiving to unwind. Little did I know that God was preparing to draw me closer to the death I sometimes desired in order to save the life He had planned for me. As I headed home to Atlanta on that cool November night, I never could have guessed God was going to wreck my life.

# 7

## Revelation
## in the Wreckage

I'm not sure how long I hung unconscious in the wreckage of my Jeep before I finally came to. I could feel the seatbelt cutting into the skin on my neck as I realized I was hanging limp and heavy like a bruised ragdoll. Warm blood drained from my mouth and seeped into my nose, choking me and causing me to gag. With each cough, I could feel more blood boil up from deep in my chest and a hot iron taste roll up behind my teeth. Desperate for breath, I squirmed and writhed, trying to relieve the pressure on my lungs. But I was pinned, strung from my seatbelt and unable to wrap my head around the balance of a world turned upside down. Every move caused more pain, so at last I stopped and hung stationary, confused even further by the exhaustion that overwhelmed me.

There was nothing echoing through the rubble but silence—a deep, peaceful silence interrupted only by the coarse and rasping breaths wheezing from me. The air was still and calm but my mind was fogged and burning. I couldn't see but I could feel. My head was pulsing and the back of my eyes were throbbing and my side was aching as I fought to breathe. I focused on what I could in my disoriented state, starting at my toes and moving each body part slowly and methodically. Ankles. Knees. Fingers. Wrists. One by one I moved each limb, blindly making sure I was all in one piece, taking a halfhearted inventory to discover the things that were hurting me. I was genuinely shocked when I realized nothing felt broken beyond repair—that my brain and my body were somehow still able to work in sync. A part of me expected to be paralyzed and I knew the intensity of the wreck should have had its way with my body. I should have been far worse off than it seemed I was. The power and force of the moments before could have so easily ended my life. For a moment I hung there in disbelief.

Wreckage. It suddenly and radically meant something new and different to me. In a moment of complete and total vulnerability—surrounded by twisted steel and fractured glass—I had never felt more at ease. In a moment that should have warranted raw, unbridled fear I felt completely at peace. A peace that met my rebellious heart and suddenly surpassed all understanding. There my body hung, with tangled and messy destruction surrounding me, sustained by something far greater than my own strength. In that moment, I was given a parallel vision of my past and my circumstances—my past just as tangled and messy as the destruction currently around me, yet my life sustained by Someone who had far greater plans and purpose for me.

That moment of perspective left my mind spinning and my heart pounding and my soul open to receive. One year prior I had been emotionally wrecked by the sudden loss of my dad.

Now I dangled, physically wrecked, broken to a place of true surrender and need. It wasn't just the rush of relief to discover I was alive that began to deeply redefine things; it was the fact that in the midst of the chaos and the brokenness I heard something very odd. A still, small voice met my heart and simply breathed, *Be still, and know that I am God* (see Ps. 46:10).

## Your Life, or Me?

I later learned that after losing control of my vehicle I'd hit an embankment and flipped my Jeep three and a half times, narrowly avoiding a steel signpost and instead slamming mid-roll into the base of a tree on the edge of a muddy hill. The impact of the crash ripped the front portion of my Jeep off and just about stripped the engine from the vehicle, leaving a mass of twisted steel and automotive debris. The Jeep came to a crashing halt on its roof, with my body trapped inside. At one thirty in the morning I hung there alone, just a few short miles from the Alabama-Georgia state line.

I must have passed out, because the next thing I knew I was on the ceiling of my car. I still don't know how I had been able to squirm from my tangled seatbelt, but I found myself sprawled atop a field of rubble and glass that littered the roof. I heard my phone's muted dings, but was too disoriented to figure out where the sounds were coming from. I sat up and realized I could see, dimly, only through my left eye. I couldn't figure out why my sight was so limited or why my right eye was throbbing, so I tried making noise in hopes that someone might see the wreck and hear me. But in my attempt to scream for help, I instead spewed hot blood. I choked and felt my throat strain and tighten. I tried to draw a deep breath in, but couldn't muster any power from my lungs.

Feeling gagged and muffled, unable to make much audible sound, I finally laid back down. It was in that rest that my mind found its way back to a place of surrender, and I immediately felt overwhelmed by a presence that was as crushing as it was cradling, as terrifying as it was all-encompassing, and as heavy as it was healing.

The presence of the Holy Spirit flowed into that wreckage mightily. And in that broken moment God chose to reveal Himself to me. The still, small voice that had whispered to my heart became an overwhelming flood of revelation as the Spirit reached deep into my calloused heart and downloaded the depth of the gospel of Jesus Christ into me.

*I. Love. You.*

*I have plans for you.*

*I have hope and purpose and life for you.*

*I created you. I sustain you. I will save you.*

*I died for you, My daughter. You are forgiven and free.*

*So choose now for yourself.*

*Your life, or Me?*

I felt peace wash over me and the arms of the King wrap around me, and not one ounce of me could make sense of why a mighty God, whom I had so carelessly sought and run from before, was dwelling in the presence of a wandering rebel like me. My mind replayed the times I had denied Him. My heart shrunk away from the thoughts of how I'd forsaken Him. My shame trembled at the doubt I had in Him and the blame I cast on Him and the hypocrisy I carried out in His name. But in the same gasping breath I felt the grace of His presence flood me. I felt forgiveness and freedom and an unrelenting peace. I saw a vision of the cross and the man who hung at Calvary. *Jesus!* In bloodied glory. Because of *my* sins He had hung on the cross, and because of *His* love He chose to die for me.

The depth of the gospel penetrated me. Humility pierced through me. A sense of security overwhelmed me. *Life* breathed through my story. Those moments in that car—they were glory. Life-saving, heart-changing, illogical glory.

It was just the Spirit of the King and I. And even though I'd heard the gospel a thousand times over and moved through confirmation and "prayed the prayer of salvation" more times than I could count, in that moment my works were irrelevant. His works were heaven-sent. My slate was wiped clean and my story turned to a new page. My name was called out by a King who knew my stubborn heart needed the isolation of a personal encounter I couldn't mute or rationalize. It was as if God knew my soul needed His undivided attention and His unbridled comfort and His personalized truth. It was as if He had willingly *wrecked my life* in order to *save my life*, and save my eternal story.

*God is beautiful.*

Those were the only three words I could process as I was pounded by the waves of His glory. His presence was crushing. His grace was unrelenting. Before I could process everything, I felt the gaping hole in my heart that longed for my earthly father filled by the love of my heavenly Father who called me His daughter and mended shut my bleeding grief with a whisper. I felt an overwhelming authenticity that required me to strip myself of all the masks and the falsehoods and the control. I felt a worth overwhelm me that fully empowered me and etched the word *beloved* deep into my soul. I also felt a boldness called from me that demanded vulnerability, and a great purpose was placed inside of me.

I felt God. I felt Jesus. I felt the Holy Spirit stifle any ounce of doubt that remained in me. And as quickly as this surge of revelation began, I also felt a calm and clarity that quieted my thoughts.

*Your life, or Me?*

As I lay there in my greatest hour, I *chose* to believe. I surrendered my life, fully, to the Author of my eternal story.

## "God Is Beautiful"

Inspired by this new hope, I sat up again, totally bewildered. My head was burning and my body was throbbing, but I felt nothing other than the will to move. To get out. To tell anyone who would listen about the King I had encountered. I felt a hunger deep within me to know more and to learn more about this amazing grace that had somehow so miraculously set me free.

Then I heard a hesitant voice stab the silence and saw a light crack through the rear driver's side window. My ears perked up and I dragged my body toward the edge of the roof as the light bounced off the shattered glass beneath me and the voice grew louder and closer. Before I knew it, I saw a man's gentle face peering into my car. He had a look of such overwhelming worry. The fear on his face looked like that of a man preparing to see a dead body. As we locked eyes in that rubble and debris, his look of shock was one of my final clear memories of that night.

The rest came in flashes—like snapshots flipping through my mind. The sight of his face. The sound of my own broken

100

voice straining to whisper to him. The cold, wet feeling as my hand reached through the shattered window and slid between blades of damp grass. The ambulance lights. And the faintest memory of my mom's voice on the other end of a telephone line telling me that everything was going to be all right.

A day or so after the crash, my mom called that man to thank him. It turns out he was one of the only other cars on my stretch of road that night. He had been driving and saw my lights flicker and swerve in the distance. Out of curiosity, he stopped to check out the scene and discovered my mangled vehicle and me. I've come to learn that God delights in orchestrating "coincidental" extraordinary things. That sometimes we can catch His splendor in the subtle, curious things. Of all the people who could have possibly come across me on that night, that man happened to be a retired paramedic and a member of the Navy. Talk about showing off—the Creator of the earth, offering a gentle, unspoken wink.

The man explained to my mom that, after finding me, he tried asking questions, tried directing me on how to escape, and tried to assess my needs, but all I kept saying were three simple words—

*God is beautiful.*

*God is beautiful.*

*God is beautiful.*

He noted that I was bloodied and beaten, but I was smiling. Continually proclaiming the beauty I'd seen. I can only imagine what I looked like to that poor guy. Swollen and scraped up and smiling like a crazy person, stumbling around trying to tell him about Jesus. Looking back, I probably should have written him a note of apology. But, hey, at least I gave him an interesting story to tell at family gatherings.

## The Road to Recovery

I awoke to the putter and beeping of hospital machines. I remember looking over and seeing a paramedic—a very cute paramedic—leaning on the wall beside my bed, staring at me. In true Mo Isom fashion, I milked the situation and stretched out my arm, signaling for him to hold my hand. He squeezed my hand and told me that he was just waiting to see me wake up, carrying out standard procedure. Determined to make the most of the moment, I said something along the lines of, "I'll never let go, Jack." Realizing I was fine—and also a fool—he dropped my hand, smiled, and left the room. No shame in my game . . . you can't blame a girl for trying.

My stay in the hospital was a blur filled with ominous machines, tedious scans, and X-rays. Needles, blood, IVs. Pain, fatigue, restlessness. My mom's and sister's arrival. My mom and sister revealing they had snuck in my dogs inside their jackets to brighten my spirits. My dogs sniffing things and barking. My dog jumping onto my fractured ribs and unhooking my IV. My mom and sister being asked to leave the hospital and remove the dogs. My mom and sister sneaking back in. We were *that* family. But the pain-filled laughs offered me some needed relief.

In the wreck I had fractured a vertebra at the base of my neck, cracked the ribs down the left side of my body, and sustained severe contusions to my lungs and liver. I had damaged my face, my eye, my jaw and, most severely, had contusions to my brain. I also jammed my pinky finger, which to this day I still say was the most painful of everything, but no one seemed to take me seriously in light of the coughed-up blood and broken neck and intense head injury. (The pinky healed, if you were wondering.)

I was severely concussed and had bruising on my brain, but I was alive. I was saved. I was renewed by a God who had boldly called me by name. I didn't have many answers, I couldn't put much into words, and I wasn't able to make sense, yet, of most things. But there was one thing I knew beyond a shadow of a doubt: I was unshakably, unmistakably captivated by my King.

# 8

## Wreck My Dependence

My physical recovery was a long and slow process. After being discharged from the hospital, I found my way home to Atlanta and then quickly back into the ER as some of the originally prescribed pain meds reacted violently with my system. Once those issues were resolved I lasted about a week in bed until my renewed and anxious heart grew restless and my type-A personality began to trump my logic—and my doctor's orders. It didn't help that my mom's type-A personality had a hard time understanding my new limitations, as well. In fact, I had only been home a few short days—with half of my face still severely swollen, a broken neck, and a motion-limiting brace strapped around me—when my mom lovingly reminded me that the Christmas tree wasn't going to decorate itself. If I was going to be spending so much time at home, I might as well knock out a to-do list. We still laugh about that to this day. I moved like a robot around the tree and groaned in pain any time I tried to reach up or bend over, as my mom questioned my poor ornament-spacing and why it was taking me so long to get the boxes empty. Whoever thought it was a good idea to leave two such ridiculously driven women alone together during a period of necessary rest and recovery clearly didn't think things through.

It didn't take much to talk my mom into letting me return to school to finish the semester and take my final exams. The academic stretch from Thanksgiving break to Christmas break wasn't very long, and the competitor in me wanted to believe I was capable of finishing what I started. I had a hard time accepting that I had significant mental and physical limitations, and I wasn't sure what would happen to my grades and my eligibility if I missed my finals. So, still riding high off the endorphins that lingered in my system following my incredible awakening, I was somehow able to pull myself together enough to ride with a friend back to the bayou and limp my way onto campus.

I lasted forty-five minutes in my first class before I passed out on my desk and woke up to the teacher staring, horrified, with very clear direction to take myself to the athletic training room. Immediately. The athletic staff wasn't thrilled to learn I had snuck my way back onto campus, and the administration had me on a flight back to Atlanta before the week's end. Fortunately, my academic advisors worked together to withdraw me from my classes, without penalty, and assured me I could make up my finals the following semester after appropriately resting through the winter holiday. I was relieved to find my way back home and into my comfy bed as the shock my body had been experiencing finally wore off and the rest my brain and body so desperately needed overwhelmed me.

I spent most of winter break sleeping and healing. But the time I was awake, the season of forced stillness finally allowed me time to reflect on the intensity of all that had happened the previous month in that Interstate 85 ravine. I couldn't believe what had become of my story. I never imagined that my arrogant and scornful cries for God to prove He was real and reveal Himself to me would have been heard, much less answered so literally. I racked my brain for a logical explanation. I tried to make sense of the situation so I wouldn't sound too crazy when I described to people what had occurred that cold November night. But in truth, I couldn't describe it simply. I couldn't rationalize its complexity. God's resuscitation of my sin-torn heart was never meant to be explained academically. It was a spiritual encounter with a holy entity far bigger than my own understanding. But there was a glorious wonder associated with the faith required to simply rest, and trust, and believe.

What I knew at the most basic level was that there was an undeniable difference between my life and my perspective before truly encountering Christ and after choosing to surrender my heart to an undeniably holy God. A newfound awareness stirred deep in me: this life was about relationship, not just religion. I was fiercely loved, no matter my past, and simply going through the manufactured motions would no longer be enough to satisfy my love-hungry soul. Knowing the right things to say and how to look a certain way meant absolutely nothing to my eternal story. Desperately working to control my life and author my own identity was as arrogant and ignorant as trying to fabricate my own glory. I began to realize that a lukewarm walk based on my emotions or my mood or my opinions was, at its core, a counterfeit faith. For far too long I had crafted a world image of "Christian" in my mind that actually looked very little like Jesus and true grace.

I had a lot of learning to do, and a lot of painful growing. I welcomed it. I wanted to know what Jesus's sacrifice on the cross actually meant for my life. I would have been the first to admit there was a lot of baggage and brokenness I'd been hiding. But even in my earliest steps of faith I began to recognize that my past wreckage no longer had the power to define me. Overcoming the adversity and scars that had defined me didn't have to be done through my own strength. I was being equipped with a newfound strength that had little to do with me—and that had the power to overcome anything. God longed to set me free. Still, surrendering my broken pieces wasn't going to be easy.

There were a few fundamental things that had been downloaded deep into my heart immediately. The first was that God the Father had created me, sustained me, and loved me fiercely. Even in the midst of my wandering and my blasphemy, there was *nothing* I had done that was outside of His forgiveness and reach. I believed He was perfect, and sovereign, and longed for me to understand that this world was only my temporary home. He had an eternity orchestrated for me, and the purpose of my days on earth were not for my own glory but to share His love with others and invite them into His eternal kingdom story.

I believed that God gave me the choice between desiring Him or desiring the things of the world. When I chose the world, my sin and my mistakes and my shortcomings had separated me from His glory. I wouldn't stand a chance against the schemes of the enemy, or have any hope for life after my time here on earth, if that sin continued to rule me and if I continued to try and be the god of my own journey. I believed God loved me *so deeply* that He made a way for mercy. He was not a furious, vindictive Father who was fed up with me. His desire for me to know Him and to live according to the purpose He had for me led Him to make a way for forgiveness and reconciliation despite everything: *Jesus*. His Son. Sent to pay the price for my failings. Sent to give His life to bridge the gap of separation and die the death I deserved. Sent not just to save me from my former ways but also to save me from an eternity of separation. I believed faith in Jesus Christ was my *only hope* in relationship and reconciliation with God Almighty.

I also believed I didn't have to take on this life alone. In Christ, God promised me a guide. I wasn't just placing my faith in a God I could hardly understand who would push me out into the world and expect me to follow His rules and be a better Christian. No, I believed I was given a Helper who made a home inside my soul when I said *yes* to God that night in the rubble. The *Holy Spirit*. My lifeline. A piece of God breathed into my heart, to comfort and direct and guide me. At the time I liked to imagine the Holy Spirit as my own personal mechanic, working on me from the inside out—slowly rebuilding my perspective and mentality. Binding together my broken pieces and graciously recrafting me. I believed that God's promise was true—that He would never leave me nor forsake me. That the Spirit within me would always see me through.

So I placed my faith in those fundamental truths. I embraced the Bible as the living, breathing Word of God that was un-questionably true. I knew I had a great deal to learn, but I felt empowered by the basic principles that were already opening my eyes to so many things I had been blind to. My heart's prayer became a repetition of a few simple requests:

*Lord, break my heart for what breaks Yours and bind my heart to Thee.*

*Give me eyes to see the world as You do.*

*Give me ears to hear the cries of others and to love them as You do.*

*Give me wisdom to separate what is of the world and what is of You.*

*Give me courage to walk in Your truth.*

*Lord, make me more like Jesus. Make me more like You.*

## First Signs of the Spirit within Me

Shortly before I returned to school for the start of the spring semester, my family and I began to notice a very odd issue that didn't seem to be going away. In fact, it seemed to be worsening with time as my brain struggled to heal from the trauma it had sustained. It started as an inability for me to verbalize some of the words I was thinking. I knew what I wanted to say, but occasionally I just couldn't quite articulate things properly. It was frustrating, to say the least, but became downright concerning when it progressed to a full-on stutter. A few confused words turned into whole sentences I couldn't articulate, and eventually I'd try to express entire thoughts but would immediately become tongue-tied.

The LSU medical team diagnosed my speech issues as a symptom of postconcussive syndrome. Then necessary appointments and activity-restrictive orders from my neurologist, in combination with extensive amounts of therapy still needed in the rehabilitation of my body, kept me off the practice field and out of several exhibition games through the spring soccer season, as our team prepared for my junior fall season. I was able to make up my final exams from the previous semester,

110

but lingering headaches and a slow mental recovery made my new academic courseload seem doubly challenging. I was still on pace with the new semester, but I found it increasingly hard to concentrate in class and complete work in the time required. And that was very frustrating.

It felt like so many of the things that had defined my identity were suddenly in question. Academically, athletically—simply my competence in day-to-day mental processing. I had held so much pride in the fact that I was such a sharp girl, typically. Now my weakness seemed to threaten everything. But while the Mo I had known would have felt out of control and struggled to desperately fix things, I was surprised when I realized that even with my "identity definers" suddenly in question, I was keenly aware of a newfound peace. It was one of the first encouraging markers I noticed of the Holy Spirit dwelling within me. A gentle reminder from somewhere within that God was in control, and that I could trust and rest in ease.

The next marker of the Holy Spirit I noticed within me was noticeably more intense and challenging. Socially, returning to my friend groups and the environments I had spent time in before my transformation was conflicting. I tried, for a while, to balance everything. I tried to step right back into the routine of my former days and to continue spending time with the same people in the same places I had hung out before. I rationalized that if I ever wanted these people to see Jesus within me, I needed to continue to stay involved with them. Maybe I could be the one to bring Christ's light into darkened places at the bar scenes and house parties and group gatherings. But the fact of the matter was that I wasn't actually ready or equipped to effectively take on those places as mission fields. I was actually just uncomfortable looking *too* different by stepping away.

My flesh wanted to stay. I didn't want to seem like the crazy Christian girl who was suddenly "too good" for these places and people. I didn't want to cause too much of a stir. Also, stepping away from my friends meant stepping out on my own. At the core, I was terrified of being alone.

So for a while I tried to juggle it all. And, inevitably, temptation and sin crept back in and caused me to stumble. But this time around there was something different inside of me, something I hadn't experienced before. A sense of *conviction* that was powerful and swift. Not guilt. Not shame. Rather an overwhelming awareness that my choices and my actions weren't bringing God praise. I quickly realized the newfound Spirit who inhabited my heart was jealous for my attention and my undistracted faith. There was a noticeable difference, to me, in the appeal of the "temporary pleasures" I used to chase.

I couldn't get the same high. Each thrill felt tacky and cheap and canned. I couldn't even turn on the radio and hear music the same way. The Spirit pressed a disdain for sin so powerfully within me that my prayer for "eyes to see the world as God saw it and ears to hear as He did" literally left me wincing, constantly. It was as if God unveiled my heart to the difference between the world and His glory. I was startled by what I saw and heard and read on the radio, TV, and internet. My newfound awareness of sin and debauchery and rebellion was almost overwhelming. I realized I had experienced a holy joy and fulfillment that ran so deeply and was so all-consuming that it made everything of the world feel manufactured and fake. The hole in my heart was mending. The temporary pleasures were far less than fulfilling.

As I sat in a Tiger Land bar one weekend, trying to blend in with my friends and not seem *too* different, I looked around and felt sad for the countless hearts I knew were empty. I found myself in the arms of a King who invited me to step away from pleasing the world for the sake of my worth and I consciously decided that a season of loneliness was worth my time if it meant being able to fully process my changed and renewed life.

## R.I.P. Me

There are countless verses laced through Scripture that call us to *die to self*. What's funny is that, many times, when we first come to know Christ we expect that death to be easy. But when I came across Galatians 2:20, something new stood out to me.

> I have been *crucified* with Christ and I no longer live, but Christ lives in me. The life I now live in the body, I live by faith in the Son of God, who loved me and gave himself for me. (emphasis added)

I started to think about Christ's crucifixion. About the sacrifice of an innocent man that was made for me. About the Son of God who could have so easily put a stop to all of the pain and suffering, but who knew there was only one just way for the price of my sin to be paid, so instead took on death and chose you and me.

When God created the earth and saw that it was good, He was already authoring our stories. When He created man and woman in His own image, He delighted in the joy of one day forming us too.

When sin entered into the world and we, as humans, chose our *own* way rather than God's way, we created a separation that ached Him deeply. But in spite of our rebellion, He still chose us and made a way for redemption in our stories.

When Jesus was born on this earth, fully God and fully man, God chose us as He unfolded His glory. When Christ began to walk through His life, turning from temptation and sin, He knew His faithful walk was all for the sake of choosing us, in the end.

When the cynics harassed and the jeering ensued and the doubters mocked and taunted, calling Him "King of the Jews," Christ bore the brunt of the world turning its back on Him and still chose us despite all that we lack. As He cried out to God in the Garden of Gethsemane and the weight of what was to come forced Him to sweat blood, He begged God to reveal to Him if there was any other way. When God made clear that there was not, Jesus chose us and stayed.

When they judged Him and made the choice to crucify Him, the most excruciating and humiliating death possible, Jesus stood as an innocent man and knew what was coming. And still chose us, rather than running. As they stripped Him and beat Him and lashed the skin off His back, He hunched over that stone and chose us, and He took a beating we can hardly fathom today.

When He was exhausted, bloodied, and beaten and they forced Him to carry His own cross up the road to Calvary, He stumbled through the crowds of jaunting and jeering and chose us with every step. As they drove nails through His hands and feet and hung Him on the cross for the world to see, they challenged Him as the Son of God and dared Him to bring Himself down. But Jesus chose us, a King in a blood-soaked crown.

With His final wheezing breaths He boldly chose *you* as He cried out to God in heaven, "Father, forgive them, for they do not know what they are doing" (Luke 23:34).

The realization of what Jesus's crucifixion actually looked like, and the fact that His anguish was the death that I deserved, changed everything for me. It was humbling. And crippling. And overwhelming. I realized that Christ didn't just die *for* my sins, He died *because* of my sins. I had to understand that, personally. Or else the gospel story was always going to seem unattached from me. I was the executioner, lashing His back. Every time I chose the world over what was righteous, I was the one striking another blow. When I knowingly sinned and chose my own pleasure over honoring God, I was the one spitting on Him and mocking Him as He carried the cross. In my sin I was the one who stood, taunting Him, on the hill of Calvary. I was the one arrogantly daring Him to prove Himself and come down. I was the one blind to the fact that the death He was dying was on my behalf. It became life-shatteringly clear to me that His crucifixion changed everything. If Jesus had died in such a way to save me, who was I to be "too uncomfortable" to sacrifice my comforts for Him every day? If I longed to die to myself and be crucified with Christ, I had to be willing to wholeheartedly carry out Luke 9:23, which reads, "Whoever wants to be my disciple must deny themselves and take up their cross daily and follow me."

I knew that stepping away from the peer groups and physical relationships and social scenes of the life I had known would be challenging, but the sacrifice of Christ warranted a response. A true response. Because God isn't in the business of editing behaviors. He is in the business of transforming hearts. And an effort to just edit my behaviors in response to Jesus's sacrifice and be a "better person" was bound to leave me as bankrupt as I'd felt before when I was chasing religion. No, Jesus's sacrifice meant something deeply significant to my heart and invited relationship that warranted a brave response. I believed that stepping out of my comfort zone and facing the scrutiny and criticism of those who didn't understand was the least I could give as the first offering to such a merciful and selfless King. A life-praise in response to Christ's incredible sacrifice for me.

### Are You Willing?

I realized what my soul desperately needed was uninterrupted one-on-one time. A voluntary season of isolation with Jesus. That's not to say I became a hermit and completely withdrew from everything around me, but I began to consciously rewire my mind to embrace the stillness and the silence and the loneliness as a welcomed escape with my King. To voluntarily wreck my dependence on the things I thought I needed to be happy.

I continued to work, academically. I continued to engage with my team and navigate through my physical therapy and healing. I continued to reach out to and love those around me, but I willingly turned down most extracurricular things. In such a noisy, stimulating, distracting culture, I chose to carve out time to reintroduce myself to me. I'm a firm believer that it's essential for every follower of Christ to walk through a season of voluntary isolation with Jesus. That, to some degree, it's necessary. To separate ourselves from the comfort of our former lives and the rhythm of our sin. Whatever that sin may be—an unhealthy relationship, a tempting or gossip-filled peer group, a drug habit or other substance abuse. God calls all of us to give up certain dependencies. To mute the noise that has filled our minds and stand still in the splendor of His presence, if just for a while, as He does necessary work within us. To flee from temptation and learn to lean into righteousness—no matter the cost. This necessary loneliness tends to be the greatest challenge for those yearning to surrender, as well as the greatest way to recognize the idols that own us.

Far too often we fall away from our faith when we realize the things between Christ and us are things we feel uncomfortable leaving. I think we'd like to believe we can find a middle ground, but compromise isn't a currency in God's economy. There is a deep and abiding need for commitment and consistency. Not because God presents a "list of rules" that we have to follow in order to know righteous living but because God created us, and loves us, and knows what is best for us. Sincerely. He asks us to surrender the idols that own us so we can first and foremost fulfill our hearts' most pressing needs. The question is rarely *what* we think we should give up. We all have things in our life we know we need to surrender. You probably have something sitting on the forefront of your mind right this minute as you read. The question God truly wants to know is *Are you willing?*

I've found that God communicates with each of us uniquely. Conviction makes us aware of our sin struggles, but it's the still, small voice of the Spirit within us that invites us to surrender those things. It's hard to explain what it feels like when God draws something to our attention or places a calling on our hearts. I find His guidance in the Word, I find it through constant prayerful dialog, I find it in the words of those around me who are rooted in Truth and who offer guidance to me. It's not as though I need to hear God speak in some booming, audible voice in order for me to know it's Him. It's when I search for His wisdom in the tiniest things that I begin to feel Him, deeply. I can recognize when God is calling me to do something because, generally, it is an idea or a thought I would never have on my own. A feeling or a motivation to do something that is so far outside of what is comfortable for me, or what our society deems "normal," that it would be easy to ignore or dismiss.

It takes a good deal of discernment to recognize what is a true calling, but the more I've grown in my relationship with God and the more I have made the sacrifices He asks of me, the more I have been rewarded and seen the fruits of His grace. His voice becomes clearer in our lives when we know Who we are listening for. It's up to us to close off the noise of the world around us and to begin to listen carefully.

As for me, stepping into such a season of focus unmasked my biggest idol *quickly*.

# 9

## Wreck My Obsession

Jesus replied: "'Love the Lord your God with *all* your heart and with *all* your soul and with *all* your mind.' This is the first and greatest commandment. And the second is like it: 'Love your neighbor as yourself'" (Matt. 22:37–39, emphasis added).

This was the first passage I came across after reading *Crazy Love* by Francis Chan and, as a result, consciously decided I wanted to begin approaching Scripture differently. I wanted to embrace it for its black-and-white, raw and real, heart-wrecking meaning. I wanted to trust that the Bible was life-breathed. Even though it was complex, even though it was daunting, there was a King-spoken peace in my heart that told me I didn't need all of the answers immediately in order to trust there was holy truth in the pages of God's story. I wanted to trust that every word carried purpose and power, and to stop rationalizing simpler or era-adjusted meaning out of verses I found hard to understand or believe. I had spent too many years going through the motions and glazing past the words and mindlessly memorizing the passages I cared to apply to my life. So much of the Bible was familiar from being "churched," but I couldn't have honestly told you why it was personally supposed to matter to me or how it was supposed to impact my life. Up until that point the Bible had served as more of a motivational quote book for me. I had listened to everyone else's interpretations or thoughts on the Scriptures but had never actually taken the initiative to study through things personally or allow God to speak to me through what I now understood was a great love letter He had written me. To be honest, up until that point I saw the Word as a source I could thumb through for Scripture that felt good and fit my needs and sounded strong enough for me to share in a Facebook status or on my Twitter feed.

But now I was gasping for truth and the holy Word was what my soul yearned desperately to breathe. I was starving for more of Jesus. Hungry to know what guidance was actually held in the Word that for so long had seemed unfamiliar to me. And my insatiable hunger for Truth, in its most raw and naked meaning, led me straight to a verse I had listened to so many times before but never truly heard. A verse about loving the Lord with *all* my heart, *all* my soul, and *all* my mind. A verse about loving, wholeheartedly, the King who had loved me first.

It had been about six months since my return to school. Six months of recovery that had seen the healing of my stutter, the strengthening of my body, clearance from the neurologist, and a strenuous journey back into athletic fighting form. In God's immaculate sense of timing, those six months had also welcomed a stint training with the U-23 US Women's National Team. I had prayed they wouldn't call me up for a camp while I was recovering. The program was fiercely competitive. If they had called while I was injured and I had to turn down an invitation to compete, that would have been the nail in my coffin with the team. Call it what you want, coincidence or irony or a perfectly orchestrated God-wink, but it was less than one week after I was finally cleared by my neurologist that my phone rang while I was studying in the school library. It was a representative from the US Women's National Team. They hadn't been made aware of my injuries, but were pleased to hear my acceptance after inviting me out to train with the U-23s in Portland for a week.

I didn't have much time to try to prepare to compete in top form, but I still made my way to the West Coast and spent a week training alongside women who now hoist a World Cup trophy. Alex Morgan, Kelley O'Hara, Christen Press, Tobin Heath. Little did I know the girls I was learning and growing with would go on to represent our country and dominate the international stage in 2015.

It felt, once again, like I was drinking water through a fire hose as every day opened new doors for all the Lord was downloading into my heart and teaching me. Like one of those awkward teenage growth spurts that happen far faster than your clothes can keep up with, my spiritual growth reminded me of my physical growth in the seventh grade. That year I had grown seven inches in one school term. The growth was great, a sign that I was thriving and healthy, but that didn't stop every inch of me from aching—my knees, my back, my neck. And now the ache was in my heart, my pride, and my unearthed dependencies.

It was somewhat overwhelming. I was grateful that I was growing so quickly in my understanding and my relationship with Christ, but I hadn't expected His pursuit of my heart to be so unrelenting. He had asked for all of my heart, all of my soul, and all of my mind, and He wasn't subtle in digging out any deep-rooted thing that was distracting me from understanding that verse in its full and abounding context. God continued to challenge me. He continued prompting surrender and, I realized in my knee-jerk moments of resistance, He was unearthing the idols that owned me.

One idol I quickly realized owned more of me than I wanted to admit was my need for the adoration and affirmation I received from men. As far back as high school, it was something I craved. Even further back than that, I'd yearned for my dad's praise. I realized that, in college, I'd always had a boyfriend or a guy I was interested in. In my deepest seasons of wandering, I'd relied on value from a sexual fix.

Over the course of several years I'd developed a dependence on the praise and worth men gave me. There was something about their pining that made me feel powerful. There was something rewarding in knowing I could tease or please or even control a man with my beauty. But what I rationalized as innocent and fun and feminine I began realizing was actually where I'd consistently turned to find value and company and fulfillment. I could feel the Spirit starting to stir something within me. I didn't know what it was, exactly, but I did know I was being prompted to hand over that deep, longing need. So my mind went to work trying to figure out exactly what God was asking of me, and it didn't take long before I realized that He meant *all of my heart* quite literally.

### Kissless Till Next Christmas

At the start of the new year, my heart came back to the concept of voluntary wreckage and I suddenly found a radical thought

122

popping into my mind. I dismissed it immediately, but this particular idea hung around. I hadn't forgotten what God had begun stirring in my heart a few months before, and the very clear Scripture I had been focused on, but this particular idea felt big. And undesirable. And intimidating.

*Try not to share even a kiss with anyone for a year.*

I'll be the first to proclaim that God has a wonderful sense of humor, but I wasn't laughing at that one. I was a twenty-one-year-old entering my senior year of college and the first argument I thought of was, *What if I meet someone along the way?* I knew God had called me to unearth and surrender my need for affirmation from men, but I wasn't expecting Him to call me into an intentional season of singleness at such an inopportune time—and especially not for so long.

I came up with every excuse in the book. My heart wanted to welcome God's glory voluntarily, but my brain wanted to talk me out of it when it was inconvenient for my story. I grappled back and forth with the thought and kept trying to shake it. I refused to take it in prayer to Him, because I was convinced that if I just didn't acknowledge it, it would go away. But God knew whom He was working with; He knew my stubborn heart. So, as I was loading up my car to head back to Baton Rouge for spring term, He smacked some sense into me with a clear sign.

As I walked upstairs to the kitchen to say goodbye to my mom, I noticed a sermon she was watching on TV. The minister was preaching on the practice of spiritual fasting. It was a new concept to me. I hadn't heard much about it and hadn't come across it in my readings. It certainly wasn't something that my family had ever actively practiced when I was growing up. I had heard of fasting from food and drink, but a disciplined spiritual fast was something totally unfamiliar to me.

I stood in the den staring at the screen and was captivated by the preacher's words. I started asking my mom question after question about the concept. What was a spiritual fast? Where does it talk about it in the Bible? Why is it done? Is it done with more than just food? How long do people generally fast? What's the point, and how would it help someone grow spiritually? My mom tried her best to answer all of my questions, but I could feel a flame of curiosity being fanned in me and I was eager for more knowledge. I was hungry to know what this man was talking about and how it pertained to me.

It wasn't long into my drive back to the bayou that I found myself in prayer.

*What do you want from me, Lord?*

*What are You asking for here?*

*I have been faithful, I have been following You, and I have been disciplined.*

*I've already sacrificed my friend group, my social scene, and my relationships.*

*I know You're doing work in me, but what more would You have me give?*

I've come to learn, in my spiritual walk, to never expect an immediate response. Patience is key when you are searching for answers. Key to a balanced sense of discernment. That's why it stunned me when, as quickly as I had cried out, He flooded my mind with an immediate response.

*I love you. I am jealous for you. I want to be the relationship you fully choose.*

*You are mine and I am Yours. I long to be your bridegroom.*

*But a monogamous relationship with Me can never be sustained if you cave to the whims of an adulterous heart.*

*So for a year I want you to delight in Me. I long for all of your heart.*

To say I was moved is an understatement. It was more like I was shattered. Humbled that God would desire such intimacy with me. I prayed He would make clear His plans and, through the rest of the drive, prayed over this new concept of fasting. By the time I pulled through the Red Stick's city limits, I knew a yearlong intimacy fast was what He was asking of me. Even though I knew close to nothing about the concept of fasting, I trusted God would teach me. So I clung to Proverbs 3:5–6, "Trust in the LORD with all your heart and do not lean on your own understanding. In all your ways acknowledge Him, and He will make your paths straight" (NASB). Again, I chose to believe.

As nervous and anxious as I was about handing over a year of my life, I was also excited for the challenge. I cleverly dubbed my mission "Kissless Till Next Christmas" and committed to a year of intimate exclusivity with Jesus. I decided to treat my relationship with God like I would treat a monogamous relationship with another person. I carried myself as if I were taken—I didn't allow my eyes to wander, I didn't flirt, and I certainly didn't give away any of myself physically. I entered into a yearlong commitment and never could have imagined all God was going to wreck in me.

**Seen. Known. Secure. Forgiven. Daughter. Masterpiece.**

It was hard, at first. The first three months of my intimacy fast felt like an eternity. The voluntary wreckage of my obsession with praise and affirmation from the opposite sex was startlingly challenging. The boldness it took to surrender my whole heart to God served to reveal my weaknesses quickly. In the first several weeks I felt vulnerable and exposed as I realized the embarrassing depth of my dependency. Like an addict detoxing, I had plenty of days where my pride ached and my heart swayed and my flesh yearned for a fix. I felt like I was catching myself constantly. I realized that flirting and teasing and exercising power were almost second nature to me. It didn't help that I couldn't turn on my computer or watch TV without something tempting or testing me. In a sex-crazed, relationship-dazed, one-night-stand culture, I became overwhelmingly aware of the nonstop triggers shaping the perspective and relationship standards in our society.

For the first time in my spiritual walk, I began to get a taste of the intentionality required of me. I suppose I had lived most of my adolescence like a game—determining my decisions or reactions as I went, on a case-by-case basis. There had always been a strategy to the games played between women and men, but the thrill of the chase had also come with the promise of guess-as-you-go spontaneity. Now I was forced to pay attention to everything. Scripture calls us to guard our hearts, to cling to purity, and to take every thought captive and submit them to Christ. What I realized quickly was this required me to be constantly aware, constantly focused, and constantly transparent with God. It was initially exhausting. But at the same time I found that with every day that successfully passed I gained confidence in embracing my small victories. As days turned into weeks and weeks turned into months, my mentality shifted from weary crawling to confident walking and eventually to bold running toward the King. I gained confidence and determination as I pressed through the year and eventually became aware of all that I was learning. The most fundamental revelation was this:

126

*in Christ I was seen, known, and secure, a forgiven daughter and a purposed masterpiece.*

———————

I began to foundationally trust that I was seen by God. Not only had He proven that to me in my car accident when He boldly and personally answered my cries and revealed Himself, but He continued to remind me of it as I learned to fix my eyes on Him daily. For a long time I had struggled with feeling like I was forgotten. Maybe you've been wrestling with feeling that way too. I didn't always feel God, or feel like I was loved by God, or feel like I had the ability to hear God like so many people talked about. For a lot of my churched youth I didn't know if I was doing something wrong or missing something, and I was too nervous I would seem foolish or inadequate if I voiced that I just didn't understand what everyone else seemed to be experiencing. Ultimately my frustration culminated into feeling like God must have forgotten me, particularly after my dad passed, and in my suffering I ran from the God whom I felt had failed me. I projected anger toward God on the surface, but in my depths I was aching because I felt like I wasn't seen.

But when I intentionally put on blinders to the world and entered into my intimacy fast, I realized I wasn't the one forgotten. I was the one who *had* forgotten, all along, to set my eyes on God. When we fix our eyes on the sovereign and omnipresent power of the King, we learn that there is never a moment we aren't sought after and wholly seen. He does reveal Himself in the big, bold productions at times, but more often than not, I learned, our God is a God of details and small things. He delights in whispers to our hearts we must be quiet enough to hear. And we must be present enough to see the subtle signs that He is with us, the frequent "coincidences" we can begin to recognize as God-ordained orchestrations. And we can notice the beauty of the world around us in His immeasurable creation.

> Where can I go from your Spirit?
>> Where can I flee from Your presence?
> If I go up in the heavens, you are there;
>> if I make my bed in the depths, you are there.
> If I rise on the wings of the dawn,
>> if I settle on the far side of the sea,
> even there your hand will guide me,
>> your right hand will hold me fast. (Ps. 139:7–10)

When I began to pay attention, I realized He was everywhere, in everything, and constantly delighting in me.

The next thing I began to realize was that I was deeply and intently known by God. I came across Psalm 139:13–14 and meditated over its truth for several months of my journey: "For you created my inmost being; you knit me together in my mother's womb. I praise you because I am fearfully and wonderfully made; your works are wonderful, I know that full well."

I believe God's works are wonderful. I also believe He created all things. So if His works are far from average or mundane or ordinary, and He formed our lives and our bodies, then what does that say about you and me?

For so long I had based my self-worth and identity in the things I could achieve. I felt valuable when I achieved success and less than good enough when I failed at or struggled with things. My perception of myself was constantly determined by the reflection of my endeavors and the response from other people I would receive. But God took that season of my life to crash through the self-absorbed mirrors that surrounded me and remind me that my self-worth hung on the cross at Calvary. I realized that the most irrelevant things in the equation were my works—and that His works meant everything in the summation of my worth. Not only had He fearfully and wonderfully created me, He had sustained me and saved me, and His works alone deserved all the glory.

To be known by God was the most glorious thing. His loving knowledge of my needs, my quirks, my strengths, and my weaknesses made the unique things about me defining factors of my beauty. It armored me to stand against any criticism or scrutiny. I was His creation—as are you. And the most beautiful assuredness of our worth blossoms out of our ability to know God and our unshakable awareness that we are known by God too.

I also came to believe that, in Christ, I was secure. Not only did my faith in Jesus secure my heavenly position for eternity but knowing I was seen and known by God helped eradicate my self-focused insecurities about things here on earth. I hadn't relapsed into my eating disorder for several years, but remnants of insecurity and overcompensated control still lingered in me. In my time alone with Jesus, though, He gave me a wake-up call about my insecurities that instantly and deeply made me ache.

I pictured myself standing in front of a mirror nitpicking my body and hating what I saw reflecting back at me. Then I pictured myself standing at the foot of the cross. Looking up at Jesus as He hung beaten and bloodied and swollen, nailed to the wood that stretched out on both sides of Him. I remembered that where He hung was the place that had previously been reserved for me. I was reminded of the price He paid to set me free. I looked up at Him as He sucked in fleeting breaths, a clear display of how much God fiercely loved me, and then I looked down and spit on the foot of the cross, snarling that what Jesus was doing just wasn't good enough for me.

That vision was gut-wrenching. And infuriating. I cried the day I pictured that, and pleaded with God to forgive me. In response He interpreted the things I had seen and clarified to me that every time I nitpicked my body, the beautiful creation He had crafted in His image, it was like mocking His ability to sculpt beautiful things. That every time I tore myself down with negative thoughts and negative words it was like staring Christ, who knowingly died to reveal to me my immeasurable value and worth, in the eyes and telling Him that the sacrifice He made wasn't good enough to make me believe the same things about myself. My insecurities reeked of arrogance. Sure, I could project it all to be about surface-level things, but the fact of the matter was, at the core, I wasn't insecure about my body. I was subtly in doubt that God was capable of creating wonderful things. I wasn't fixated on control; I was overcompensating for the fact that I subtly doubted God was big enough and sovereign enough and loving enough to orchestrate things as they unfolded.

My insecurities were rooted in a deep and bleeding heart condition that I had to surrender. So I clung to the Word as I wrecked my anxious fears and leaned into the truth that, in Christ, I was *secure*. And He was seated in a position higher than me and fully in control. "Have I not commanded you? Be strong and courageous. Do not be afraid; do not be discouraged, for the LORD your God will be with you wherever you go" (Josh. 1:9).

One of the most transformative fundamentals I learned as I walked hand-in-hand with Jesus was that I was also forgiven—fully.

There was so much I had kept hidden in the dark. My sexual sin still held me in a stranglehold. Even though I was walking through a season of purity and celibacy, that didn't erase the bondage and heart-ties that still lingered from my reckless promiscuity. If anything, this season of intentionally battling those triggers and temptations and desires in myself made me intensely aware of how easily I had handed myself away before. My sexual sin had to be dealt with head-on if I ever wanted to understand the deep value of purity when this fast drew to a close. If I wanted to live differently, I had to tackle the things that had previously made me live similarly to the world around me.

For a while bringing so much embarrassing messiness to the throne was intimidating. But God quickly reminded me that surrendering my messiness was the whole point of the journey. That it was a messy King-story encountering a messy me-story with the promise that it would all come together for His glory, in spite of everything. Besides, it wasn't as if He had been absent when everything happened. He reminded me I had always been seen—even in the times I'd rather not have been. So I drudged it up from the depths of my darkness and brought it all before Him. The masturbation I struggled with, the pornography I'd steadily sought out after being exposed to so much so young. The power I enjoyed over men. The promiscuity. The lack of understanding about the difference between virginity and purity and how I'd waved a pompous flag of forged virginity for so long. I brought it all before Him and He slowly coaxed more out. With each confession I felt encouraged to bring more and more, and I spent months processing and surrendering low-lying sin even I had forgotten about.

At times I felt that at some point God's grace was bound to wear out. But His Word proved to be true as He continued to wash me with forgiveness and mercy, and teach me about what sex meant to Him and how He desired the protection of my body and heart to righteously play out. "If we confess our sins, he is faithful and just and will forgive us our sins and purify us from all unrighteousness" (1 John 1:9). I was forgiven, *fully*. I knew that beyond a shadow of a doubt. I learned that there may have been discipline and repercussion for my sin, but bringing it before God in humility was the only way to weed out the guilt and bondage to shame.

It was also liberating to learn that I was a daughter of God Almighty. I had struggled so much with feeling alone and like an orphan. I had a wonderful mother, of course, and family that loved me so deeply it hurt. But the aching thought never left me that my dad's love for me wasn't enough. That my own father's love for me couldn't change the outcome of the day he left us. And that I was an orphaned daughter who would never regain the love of a father now that my dad had chosen to end his story.

You can imagine how much it wrecked me when I came across verse after verse that reminded me how God actually saw me.

I will be a Father to you, and you will be my sons and daughters, says the LORD Almighty. (2 Cor. 6:18)

So you are no longer a slave, but God's child; and since you are his child, God has made you also an heir. (Gal. 4:7)

Now if we are children, then we are heirs—heirs of God and co-heirs with Christ, if indeed we share in his sufferings in order that we may also share in his glory. (Rom. 8:17)

But you are a chosen people, a royal priesthood, a holy nation, God's special possession, that you may declare the praises of him who called you out of darkness into his wonderful light. (1 Pet. 2:9)

I was not a wandering orphan. I was not abandoned or alone. I may have been failed by my earthly father, but I had a heavenly Father who was eagerly waiting to welcome me home. Realizing I had been adopted by the Maker of the heavens and the earth put my earthly abandonment into perspective and helped heal a gaping hole in my scorned heart. I was not a wanderer. I was a daughter of the King.

Lastly, I became overwhelmingly aware that I was a purposed masterpiece. God gave me a great vision of our lives as mosaics, and reminded me that he was the Master Artist, refashioning us all. I will never forget the day He painted the most beautiful image of His handiwork in my mind: I saw my life as a child as a clean pane of glass, without blemish or scrape or flaw. When sin and brokenness and suffering entered my story, I watched the glass crack and shatter. The eating disorder, the suicide, the accident. All of the adversity and wreckage sent pieces crumbling. But then I saw God gather up the pieces and take them to a strong, stable workbench. I watched Him lay out the shards of my broken, fractured life, and begin to sift through them as if He had a vision in mind. One by one He picked up the pieces and slowly crafted them back together, but when He stepped away and revealed His work He hadn't restored me into a clean pane like before. Instead, He had formed a beautiful mosaic that His light could shine through and reflect and refract to reach people and places it never could have before. The base of the mosaic was a foundation of sturdy truth. The glue that held the pieces together was a binding of forgiveness and grace. But the most beautiful thing about the entire masterpiece wasn't just the color and light. It was the shape of the mosaic He had formed from all of my brokenness: it was the cross of Jesus Christ.

"For we are God's handiwork, created in Christ Jesus to do good works, which God prepared in advance for us to do" (Eph. 2:10).

I knew, without a doubt, that God was doing good work in my life. And I, as His beautiful handiwork, was given the privilege of doing good work in response. We are masterpieces whom He has plans and purpose for. When we accept that blessing and responsibility, our lives become abundantly more meaningful.

God desires, above all else, for us to put Him first and to love Him fully, and for our hearts to be completely satisfied in and by His love. He desires for us to know our worth in Him so that we can fully love ourselves and be able to love others righteously. In wrecking our obsessions and inviting us into a place of blind trust, God is ultimately welcoming us to learn our identity in Him—and our worth.

He taught me, so clearly, the value of making sacrifices in order to identify myself with Christ, so I was excited when I felt Him peeling back another layer and calling for the next degree of trust. But even my excitement couldn't have prepared me for the shock I felt when I learned where He intended that new journey to start. I was stunned when I realized He was clearly laying LSU football on my heart.

# 10

## Wreck My Pride

All too often, we play it safe. We tend to be just courageous enough, in our own eyes, when there's not too much at stake. We like to rationalize our more calculated public choices as careful moves to protect our purpose when, in actuality, we live in cautious timidity to protect our perception and pride. In a society where failure seems forbidden and risk is rarely encouraged if it seems to outweigh its reward, we've forgotten that we're actually invited to live boldly in the name of Jesus. And that doing so can be outrageously fun. Messy, risky, and scary—yes. But gloriously fun. God knows our hearts, knows our passions, and knows the unique platforms and plans He has for each of us. Maybe rather than being afraid we'll fall, it's simply up to us to say yes and answer His call.

When God first whispered *football*, I couldn't help but hesitate. His words had almost been audible that afternoon as I showered off the dirt and grime from my senior season's soccer practice. I knew God desired me to live fearlessly and boldly, in faith, but I thought for sure I was misunderstanding what He was asking of me that day. My type-A personality was used to safe, calculated choices. I liked to know the outcome and count the cost. I liked to be sure my investment and time in an endeavor would be worth the reward, for my pride's sake if nothing else. Apparently, God was adamant this had to change and was determined to wreck every ounce of pride and assurance I placed in my own strength.

I wasn't sure how all the pieces were supposed to line up, but there was something about the thrill of saying yes to God and taking a leap of bold faith that excited me. If I wanted to practice what I preached and truly live boldly, navigating the idea was at least worth a try. After all, what was the worst that could happen? (Besides, you know, that I could be hit by a three-hundred-pound lineman and die.) When I got out of the shower I called my mom to explain what was on my mind. She playfully reminded me that as soon as I was flattened like a pancake after a bad snap I was going to regret that bold faith. But she never questioned my resolve. Nor did she doubt that such a radical challenge could have only come from God.

I knew my circumstances were unique. LSU soccer and football had always shared a weightlifting and indoor training facility, so I had been around the football staff and players for years. My particular affinity for strength training and my constant commitment to extra voluntary workouts on my own was well known around the facility. Football Ops was my second home. I had built relationships there and proven my work ethic, and was an All-American who garnered respect, particularly in my senior season. I was also six feet tall and close to two hundred pounds of muscle at the time. It was not as if I were an incoming freshman haphazardly deciding I wanted to try out for the football team. I was a groomed and disciplined athlete, and the football staff knew me. But even still, I wasn't sure if they'd humor me, or even hear me out, as a woman seeing if I could work my way onto a man's team.

I had so many questions and uncertainties. Logistically, I didn't see how the endeavor was even a possibility. I knew that every NCAA athlete was granted five years of eligibility but was only allowed four seasons in one sport. This rule took into account if a player needed to redshirt, or sit out a season, for academic or health reasons. I had moved through my soccer career without the need to redshirt a season, and was now in my fourth year of eligibility. So, technically, I did have a fifth year to compete, and it made sense to me that the only other athletic feat I could even stand a chance to learn quickly was how to use my powerful leg to kick a pigskin properly. Academics were another question. I was set to get my undergraduate degree after the fall 2011 semester since I had come into college a semester early. How would I maintain my academic eligibility? And what would it look like in regard to my scholarship money? I had so many questions and so many doubts, so I tried to slow down and started by simply reaching out to some people I thought might have a few answers.

I texted a friend of mine who was a kicker for the team to rack his brain about whether or not he even thought the situation was a possibility. When he excitedly encouraged me to go for it, I reached out to a few other guys on the team I was close with. I was shocked when they all voiced their support. And doubly shocked when one of them questioned why I was even hesitating.

Why was I hesitating? I was hesitating because God was calling me to something I wasn't sure I could even achieve. And that something wasn't subtle. It was huge and it was daunting and it would force me onto a national platform. That terrified me. I was relatively young in my faith walk and such exposure would be challenging. I had a past and I had scars and I had a story. I was sure if I was thrust into such controversial media spotlight—particularly being a woman trying to break into a man's sport—that my past would rear its ugly head and destroy me. Not to mention LSU was the number-one ranked football program in the nation at the time. Who was I to think I could even stand toe-to-toe with men who had trained their whole lives to compete at that level? I was hesitating because the call of boldness God placed on me seemed too huge. Of all the baby steps we could have taken into this boldness, why football at LSU?

Still in denial that I was hearing God's call correctly, I nevertheless began to go through the motions of seeking approval, certain I would hit a closed door somewhere along the way. I approached the strength and conditioning coaches first. When they voiced their support, they pointed me in the direction of the administration. I met with the assistant athletic director for football operations and was stunned when he walked me through how the logistics would play out. I still had my senior soccer season to complete, but if I was willing to try and learn the kicking position and train for a year and a half before I was eligible to try out, they would see what they could do. Because of timing and eligibility, I would only have one short season to suit up, if I were to eventually make the team. But in the meantime, since I was already an athlete at LSU, I was given the go-ahead to lift weights and train alongside the team, to a certain extent, leading up to those tryouts.

I couldn't believe what I was hearing. I felt like I was in the twilight zone. I finally voiced the elephant in the room and asked him about his thoughts on the fact that I was a woman. I hesitantly reminded him about Katie Hnida, a female who had kicked for Colorado and then New Mexico in the early 2000s. In 2004 Hnida alleged that she had been molested and raped by teammates during her time at Colorado, but she never pressed charges. I wanted to make sure he'd thought through the stigma my endeavor could carry. But before I could even complete my thought, he interrupted me to remind me this wasn't Colorado, it was LSU. If I was good enough to be a proven weapon for the team, they'd make a way for me. He went on to clarify that there'd be no special treatment. That if I was going to pursue this, the final decision would have nothing to do with my gender and everything to do with my leg. This was solely about performance and skill. The best kickers would kick. So I had a lot to prove.

Academically, it was decided that if I wanted to maintain my eligibility after finishing my undergraduate degree, I would need to enroll in a graduate program. It was necessary that I be an active student through the spring term, which stretched from the end of my soccer eligibility to the time of football tryouts. If I did not make the team, I could simply wrap up my graduate studies after that one semester, but if I did make the team I would be able to continue taking graduate classes through that fall semester of football competition and beyond, if I chose. I spent time mapping out a graduate course load that would be best suited to balance with my athletics and set my mind to making it work. Graduate school wasn't something I had really ever considered before, but I was willing to do whatever it took to remain eligible and able to compete.

From there it seemed seamless as I moved through the ranks. The new special teams coach approved. Even the head football coach, Les Miles, gave the go-ahead when I brought it before him one afternoon. I felt like what God was weaving together was progressing too smoothly to be true. But I finally embraced it, and set my mind and heart to see the journey through. My prayer had consistently been, *God, if I'm misunderstanding things here and this isn't of You, please slam doors in my face and make it abundantly clear that I'm off-base.* So when it seemed like, logistically, a red carpet was being rolled out in front of me, I committed to give 100 percent of myself to the endeavor. Even when the risk of failing terrified me.

I knew immediately that a Word-honoring focus was, again, going to need to be my priority. That God's instruction knew what was best for me. I wasn't naive. As a woman, if I wanted to earn this team's respect I had to first respect myself, fully. Stepping into an environment with ninety college-aged guys from all different backgrounds and walks of life was going to require me to focus, constantly, on godly intentionality. Intentionality in how I talked, how I joked, how I behaved. Intentionality in how I dressed. Even so far as intentionality in what area in the weight room I used to stretch. The last thing I wanted was to be a distraction. The weight room, training room, and practice fields were these guys' sanctuaries. They were already being accommodating in allowing me to join the mix. I certainly did not want to be a stumbling block that stood out or drew attention or disturbed the team dynamics.

Through summer 2011 I stayed at school and juggled training for both soccer and football. I made friends with the equipment managers and showed up every other day asking for footballs and tees. Eventually they just started leaving the door unlocked and a mesh bag of equipment waiting for me. Between summer classes I showed up every afternoon along with the incoming football freshmen and the returning NFL guys who would regularly come back to the LSU facilities to train in their off season. On Mondays, Wednesdays, and Fridays we'd lift weights. On Tuesdays and Thursdays we'd run. Ladder drills, cone drills, mat drills, and sprints. Then for every time someone had jumped the line, we'd wrap up training with up-downs on the boiling turf as penance. Everyone out in that Louisiana heat had a spot on the roster and a requirement to attend—except for me. I was the only one out there by choice, with nothing more driving me than the fact that I was determined. I slowly started to gain respect among some of the guys and worked my way up to joining sessions with the upperclassmen. When I was finally training alongside, and keeping up with, the likes of Odell Beckham Jr. and Jarvis Landry and Alfred Blue, I eventually found I had also earned a spot in the rotation with the other kickers, a few times a week, when we would train on our own.

Some of the other specialists rallied behind me in my efforts and were gracious enough to lend me their time and their coaching tips as I adjusted to a wildly different kicking form. Even the special teams coach would find his way onto the indoor field when he spotted me training. *Head down, chest up, lock out your leg, and skip through.* Kicking a football was so different from kicking a soccer ball. Getting initial height on the ball so it wouldn't get blocked proved to be harder than it looked. I felt like I was slowly progressing and learning, and I watched my accuracy gradually improve and my distance gain consistency as, yard-by-yard, I worked my way further back. Practicing my kicking and working out with the guys proved to be great cross-training for soccer, and I gained strength and agility and quickness that carried me into August.

As an added bonus, the guys I'd grown friendships with on the football team jumped on board to have some fun in a series of YouTube videos that soccer's marketing team and I dreamed up to promote both sports' games in the fall. We called the series "Meaux vs." and decided I would take on certain members of the football team, one-on-one, in a series of funny competitions. A football challenge, a soccer challenge, and an off-the-wall tie-breaker if it was needed. I knew it would be fun to improvise with the guys and allow our fans to see our personalities off the field and out from behind the media's mic, but I never expected the videos to become so popular and gain so much momentum overnight. I took on the likes of Tyrann Mathieu, Russell Shepard, Zach Mettenberger, and Brad Wing, and Tiger fans ate up the excitement of seeing their favorite players compete with each other. (And I enjoyed the smack-talk as I wiped the floor with them in certain competitions!)

## A Season of Blessing

In the fall, I fully shifted my focus to my senior soccer season and squeezed in a few football workouts when I could. But I was determined to wrap up my career with the LSU soccer team on a high note and give back to the program everything it had given me through my amazing four years at the school. In fall 2011 my class claimed our third SEC Western Division championship and at-large berth into the NCAA Tournament. We also rounded things out by earning a runner-up finish in the SEC standings for the third time in four seasons. Personally, I tied for the SEC lead with eight shutouts on the season and finished my career in goal by holding the school record for all-time wins (43), shutouts (30), saves (235), and goals against average (0.86). I also finished my tenure ranked #4 on the SEC's all-time list with those 30 blank slates.

The feeling of my personal and private life finally mirroring the steady, positive performance of my athletic persona on the surface was beyond fulfilling. For the first time in a long time, I felt like my character was finally consistent between what I showed the public eye and what was behind closed doors. The masks I'd hidden behind for so long were gone. Walking hand-in-hand with the Lord no longer looked like a mistaken guarantee of blessing and provision and a nervous apprehension for what I would believe if things got hard or trying. Rather it looked like a peace-filled relationship that brought assuring hope and glory to God through all of the highs and through all of the defeats. I felt that, for the first time, Christ's light was actually able to shine through me. People were beginning to take notice of all the authentic changes in me. With my feet on solid ground and my heart blanketed in Christ's security, I found the courage to open up about my broken past and begin sharing my story.

Socially, I was beginning to build community with new friend groups that were genuine and authentic and focused on the same priorities that now lead the way in my life. The Fellowship of Christian Athletes on LSU's campus was growing like crazy, and realizing there were other college athletes around me who were dedicated to keeping Christ standing firm at the center of their lives was beyond encouraging. I began traveling throughout Louisiana sharing my testimony, and God began planting a seed of bold communication that I could feel growing.

That semester was so special as I found God pouring out affirmation and blessing I had hardly even realized my heart needed. I had been honored a short while before with the nationally recognized Wilma Rudolph Student-Athlete Achievement Award and LSU's Eye of the Tiger Award, but the kind honors continued as I was named one of the ten finalists for the 2011 Lowe's Senior CLASS Award, earned my second selection to the SEC academic honor roll, and was somehow, by some ridiculously absurd stroke of luck, voted LSU's homecoming queen that fall.

I still can't quite explain how that all unfolded. No female athlete had ever been crowned before, and I'm pretty sure it was the popularity of the "Meaux vs." videos that somehow prompted enough people to cast a vote my way. If there was one thing I learned from that night in Death Valley, being crowned in front of ninety thousand screaming Tiger fans, it was that walking on a rutty football field in four-inch heels was way harder than kicking a football through the uprights could ever prove to be.

### Boldness in the Face of Scrutiny

When that fall finally drew to a close, I hardly had time to mourn the closing of a massive chapter in my life with soccer. I hadn't heard back from the US Women's National Program since the camp following my accident. The Women's Professional League, at the time, was really struggling. I knew I didn't have the desire to travel overseas to play, so I accepted my circumstances and shifted my energy to the other sport I was learning to play. I was able to focus all of my athletic commitment on football and, even though the fall tryout that would count for me was still more than half a year away, I was welcomed to come to the spring tryout to gauge where I was, what I needed to work on, and how I stood up against other prospective walk-ons.

144

I figured the tryout would come and go without much commotion, seeing as how it was a practice run for me. We had
worked hard to keep my endeavor under wraps. But when a
group of reporters finally caught me and a few of the guys
training one day in the indoor facility, the cat was out of the
bag and a national firestorm commenced. It seemed like there
was hardly a sports TV network, radio station, or social media
site that didn't pick up on bits and pieces of my story. With the
media attention came the interest. With the interest came the
divided opinion. With the divided opinion came every sports
lover's overwhelming and adamant input into my motives, my
ability, my strengths, my weaknesses, my intentions, my faith,
my past, my present, my future, and the fact that I had a sports
bra strapped to my chest rather than a jock strap between my
thighs.

In conjunction with the LSU Athletic Administration crew,
we worked to hyperselectively pick through hundreds of media
requests to handle the necessary evil of publicly addressing the
endeavor. We agreed on a handful of outlets, I gave a few inter-
views, and then I got back to work. From that point forward,
media stations aired, reaired, and shared my story, and the nation began to pick apart, evaluate, and dig deeper into all they
were convinced they knew about "Mo Isom: the girl trying to
play football at LSU." All the while, Mo Isom, the girl trying
to play football at LSU, was simply doing just that. And was
trying to stay out of view.

A part of me was mortified. I had worked so hard to blend
in and avoid being a distraction. The unnecessary attention was
overwhelming. It proved to reinforce why I had been hesitant
to begin the journey in the first place. Training with the team
before had been easy. But now camera crews followed me around

on the indoor field and made some of the guys annoyed. I had to come home each day to read blogs and forums and websites constantly praising, scrutinizing, or analyzing me. My height, my weight, my figure, my body. It seemed as though my open faith was one of the biggest hot-button topics surrounding me too. So many people had an opinion about my outspoken biblical views.

I think the hype of the college football culture in our country often blinds people to the reality that the players are just a bunch of kids—kids who navigate their way through college classes, fumble through the highs and lows of relationships, and ultimately play the sports they love for the schools they're awfully proud to represent. In those respects I fit right in with my gridiron brothers. There was nothing unique or outrageous that divided us. We were all athletes working our hardest to push ourselves beyond the limit of "normal." My pursuit of a football career was no different than theirs. I didn't quite understand why my personal walk with Jesus seemed to be so polarizing to the outsider looking in.

For the first time in my football journey I realized a piece to the bigger picture of what God had called me to. A part of me knew it never could have been as simple as making a football team. God had also been building a platform for me that He trusted I would use to give Him glory. That was a pivotal learning lesson in calling me to live boldly, as it should be for all of us. He doesn't just call us to big and bold things for the experience alone. He calls us to the radical so we can discover our courage and our voice and grow.

It seemed like those on the outside who were plugged in to my football endeavor had divided into three camps: those who fully supported my faith and were proud to see me bringing God glory through such a vulnerable endeavor, those who despised the public proclamation of God's grace in my story and wanted nothing more than to see me fail—often tossing out the cheap shot and saying I just wanted "fifteen minutes of fame," and those who could have cared less about the faith side of things and were just interested in the sports story that was unfolding.

In trying to navigate the newfound attention, and often feeling like I'd rather disappear than continue to face so much public dissention, I came across a piece of Scripture that reminded me of a hard but freeing truth. John 15:19 simply reads, "If you belonged to the world, it would love you as its own. As it is, you do not belong to the world, but I have chosen you out of the world. That is why the world hates you."

I wished I could have appeased everyone, but a bold faith rarely warrants a mild response. The Bible reminds us that many people despised Jesus. If we truly want to look like Christ, we have to come to terms with the fact that many people will despise us too. If we spend our lives compromising ourselves to try and ensure everyone around us stays satisfied, we'll find we stand for nothing and that we'll desperately be chasing counterfeit happiness all of our lives. We're called to stand boldly and surrender our comfort for the sake of righteous and unfailing truth. So I put my nose to the grindstone, drowned out the noise around me, stood firm in God's calling, and let my life be living proof.

I trained through the rest of the spring and found myself focused and ready to finally try out come fall. Over the course of my eighteen months of preparation, the dynamics of the roster had changed so much. Where there had been a real need for kickers when I first began my journey, there were now four other specialists and two additional recruited walk-ons, each likely to redshirt (meaning to sit out from competition for a year in order to prepare and develop more without losing a year of eligibility), set to join the team. The returning starter was a senior coming off an All-SEC year, so no one was beating him out. But even though I recognized the odds were stacked against me, I was still focused on giving it all I had.

I wanted to earn it. I didn't want anything given to me. I had done all I could possibly do to prepare to that point. So when tryout day finally came and I sat on that hot metal bench and laced up my cleats, I took a deep breath and finally, fully, surrendered the pride and need for control within me.

## The Answer We Don't Expect

The AC hummed as Coach Miles slowly crafted his words. There was a mutual understanding that hung thick in the room. A mutual respect. He knew all I had been through—it was an unspoken reality that demanded respect, for the commitment alone. He knew of my personal journey—the suicide of my father, the horrific car accident—and he knew of my recovery, of my unflinching commitment to live life unchained by my adversities. He knew all that I had voluntarily, physically endured for eighteen months—the three-a-days, the strict nutritional regimen, the weight training program, the injuries, the rehabilitation, the countless hours of work on my own. He knew that I had successfully navigated the obstacles of being a woman in a man's environment—that there had never been issue or controversy, and that the team respected and accepted me. He knew that I had handled the media carefully, that I had garnered support from thousands as well as faced constant

148

scrutiny and degradation by uninformed yet overly confident outsiders. He knew all of those things.

I knew he had a difficult decision to make. I knew he had given me a fair opportunity—an open door and open access to his facilities, his coaches, his equipment, and his program. I knew he had also faced scrutiny and, likely, some distraction in the process. I knew he had a unique situation on his hands and that he had never complained, asked me to leave, or discouraged my goal. He had always encouraged me, always supported me, and always granted me the opportunity to try for my dream.

He had also always been honest with me. That final day, sitting in his office, was no exception. It was not easy news to hear, as I'm sure it was not easy news to deliver. After eighteen months of effort, nobody wants to hear a no. But no was the final verdict. I had to hold my head high, though my brow quivered and my face grew hot.

As thoughts and emotions swirled through my mind, I worked to process all that I was feeling. Coach Miles continued to talk, and while I was trying desperately to listen and process his words, I found myself zoomed out of my circumstances and overwhelmed by the weight of his goal-ending word.

No. Though I could strike fifty-three-yard field goals, there were other guys already on the roster who could do the same.

No. Though I was consistent, accurate, and conditioned, there was not room or need for another specialist that particular season.

No. Though I had worked for a year and a half, extended my college education into the graduate program, and perfectly structured my course load moving forward, I would not be competing for one more fall.

No. Though the nation was on edge waiting to hear the result—though I wanted to prove right all those who believed in me and disprove all those who had doubted and degraded me—the story was at its end.

No. Though I believed that God had specifically called me to pursue this goal, the final verdict was no.

No.

In the weeks that followed, I found myself confused, agitated, anxious, and somewhat depressed. All I had invested in was stripped away. All I had been driven by and motivated toward would never come to exist. Not only was I not on the team but I was no longer a student-athlete. My eligibility was done. My college career was over. I questioned what more I could have done. I replayed every step and every kick from my tryout in my mind. I questioned Coach Miles, I questioned the motives of the decision, and I questioned whether I had ever really had a chance at all. I questioned the system. I had seen how things truly worked from the inside, and I questioned the process. I grieved over the loss of my dream. I grieved over my failure. I grieved over the no.

Time and time again I was drawn back to the same exasperated and frustrated question. *God, I believed that You specifically called me to this chapter of life. Was I mistaken all along? Was I just wasting my time? Am I the fool? Were those who doubted me right? If You called me to take on this challenge, and You saw how diligently and passionately I worked toward it in Your name—always giving You the glory—wasn't it Your will for me to ultimately make the team?*

And for the second time in a month, I was hit with the most rattling, course-altering answer. *No.*

The resounding no that was now echoing in my heart gradually pushed out the doubt, anger, and resentment that had been brooding there. This no was humbling, precise, and revelatory. It drew me to a realization of a reality that I suppose I was intended to learn, all along. No was not a word of dismissal, it was a word of direction.

I was called to listen to God's leading, take on the challenge He presented me, and passionately pursue the goal He set, in Christ's name. I was never assured of the result. Would I have been as willing to take on such a crazy, vulnerable, and challenging feat had I known there was a closed door at the end of it all? No. Yet God had reason for every step of my journey. Was it up to me to worry about whether those who had doubted me were arrogantly walking around with the false presumption that they had been right all along and knew all the details of the situation? No. Their hearts and their humility were in God's hands. Was I a fool for having tried and having believed in myself? No. I was strengthened, nourished, and matured through the process. Was I a failure for having received a no? No. *The success was not in the outcome but in the steps of faith it took to complete the journey.*

If my journey with the LSU football team taught me anything, it was that there was power in listening to God's call and responding to it. His direction looks different in each of our journeys, but we can't hold a narrow-minded and presumptuous misunderstanding that God can't use us on a day-to-day basis unless He is using us in an extreme way. As if earthly success is equivalent to our overall effectiveness. God yearns to use us daily, in every form, fashion, and function. We aren't asked to box God into the ways we think He can and can't use us. He works across a spectrum, far beyond our understanding, to align each of our steps with perfect purpose. His call in your life is going to be something tailored to exactly who you are, through your strengths, your talents, and your design. Allow Him to stir your heart and guide your steps.

It is not up to us to fully grasp the outcome before we ever commit to the challenge. It's not up to us to worry or stress about the elements of the process we can't control. It's simply up to us to move forward and to trust in God's provision and direction—knowing along the way we are bound to hit both big and small nos. Though I'd been conditioned to believe a closed door after a committed journey meant I'd fallen short, our loving King reminded me He'd used every moment of the ride. No was not a word of dismissal but a word of direction through the surrendering of my pride.

# 11

## Wreck My Plans

"Take delight in the LORD, and he will give you the desires of your heart" (Ps. 37:4). I think we often read this verse with the idea that, *if* we are faithful, God will give us whatever we want, when in actuality it is reminding us that *when* we are faithful and delight in Him, what *He* wants for our lives becomes our desires as well. His purpose and plans intertwine with our hearts, and the course we never mapped becomes the course we're eager to start.

I had always planned on a career in sports journalism. From radio and television work during my childhood to majoring in broadcast journalism at LSU, I took every step to ensure I would have the best possible résumé lined up once I finished school. The viral success of my "Meaux vs." YouTube series seemed like an added bonus, and just about everyone I knew was sure it wouldn't be long before I was sitting behind an ESPN desk.

I initially figured that my experience in public speaking was just another valuable tool in my broadcasting belt. Once I had processed all that had happened to me and all the Lord had done in my life, I began sharing my testimony around Baton Rouge. It started as a few small engagements here and there—community service hours when I volunteered to speak to Sunday school classes or small groups that reached out to me. I started my blog a short while before that time, and my dramatic personal story, in conjunction with the fact that I was an LSU athlete, stirred up some interest in local circles. One speaking engagement led to another, and before I knew it my calendar was spotted with engagements all around town, prompted solely by word-of-mouth. I spoke at sorority functions and to campus clubs, at nearby churches and to civic organizations in town.

I didn't think much of the doors God was opening, initially. I knew there was something I loved about stepping on stage and sharing my heart—something deeply special about looking through the eyes of the audience and connecting with the stories of those listening. I could tell God had blessed me with a special gift of articulation and storytelling, but there was no connection in my mind, at the time, of how my love for writing and speaking—for boldly communicating the gospel—could be used in a bigger capacity. So I chalked up my events as great experience and continued to balance them into my schedule as I studied and competed through the remainder of my school years.

In August 2012, after Coach Miles's no, I decided to withdraw from graduate school and head home to Atlanta in search of a job. I knew it would be beneficial to live back in a bigger city for a while. Half of me figured it was a wise career move and could open up doors with CNN or Turner Broadcasting or another big-market station in the South. The other half of me just desperately wanted some time back home near my sister and my mom. Life had been such a whirlwind through the past several years that we had never really had the chance to spend any length of time together as grown women. So I sold all of my possessions, gave the check to my friend who was support-raising to go into the mission field on the World Race, got baptized in a rehabilitation pool underneath Tiger Stadium, and packed up my two dogs. I headed back to the place I had left so many years before in such a broken state, now a completely new woman brought to life by God's immeasurable grace.

I spun my wheels for a long time, trying to knock down doors on the broadcast side of things. The job hunt was frustrating, to say the least. On paper, I seemed to have all the pieces in place, and in person, as many people noted, I carried an intangible quality and on-camera strength. But the industry was competitive and, for whatever reason, the opportunities just weren't happening for me. Meanwhile, I continued to receive speaking requests. My platform was beginning to spread from Louisiana to more of the Southeast. I didn't exactly understand how people were hearing about me. I wasn't doing any marketing, I wasn't sharing on social media that I was even available to come and speak, and I had no type of business model set up to handle the logistics. But dots kept connecting and word kept spreading, and before long I realized I was traveling almost constantly. I loved speaking. Every group I connected with seemed to breathe new life into my anxious soul. Pouring myself out on stage and sharing the gospel night after night was gloriously exhausting. I found that when I went to bed those particular evenings, I felt a fulfillment that was uniquely satisfying.

Still, this wasn't my "real" career plan. If anything, it was an enjoyable extracurricular activity. I had imagined and mapped out exactly what I wanted to be doing. And, to be transparent, the notoriety and recognition of a broadcasting gig was part of what I was pursuing. I felt, in many ways, like people expected me to make an immediate splash into the sports broadcasting scene. I was frustrated that the position I felt God had opened so many doors for, and for so much of my life, was suddenly so inaccessible to me.

After a few months I was finally presented an opportunity with ESPN. They had flown me out to their studios in Bristol, Connecticut, once before, but nothing much had unfolded from those meetings, so I was thrilled to be invited out again. I was set to fill in for the female host on a show called ESPNU UNITE, but I couldn't shake an unsettled feeling that lingered in me. My first night on the show I felt completely off. I couldn't figure out what was wrong. Quite literally, I was standing in the midst of my wildest dreams. Everything I had hoped for and worked toward was right in front of me and I didn't want to take for granted an opportunity that I knew so many women would have given much to achieve. But I'll never forget one particular moment standing in the studios the second night. I'd worked out the jitters from the night before. My hair and makeup had been done, I'd spent a great afternoon working alongside the cast and crew, and I felt more familiar with the flow of the show and all that I was supposed to do. That's why I was stunned when, as I stared into the lens of the camera as the teleprompter counted down the seconds until we were set to go live, I finally realized, deep down within me, that this wasn't what God was calling me to do with my life.

When I got back to my hotel room after the show I could hardly sleep. I felt conflicted by all of the thoughts and the emotions I was wrestling with. I wanted to follow God's will but I had no idea what He was trying to tell me. It genuinely terrified me that, as I was standing in the midst of my dreams, He would call for the wreckage of my plans and stir a restlessness so deep within me. I didn't know what my next move was supposed to be. I flew home to Atlanta and spent a week grieving the surrender He was asking of me. Then I spent the next few weeks trying to figure everything out and come up with solutions and remap my plans for my future.

When I was mentally and emotionally exhausted, someone finally suggested to me that if I wanted answers perhaps I should actually set my gaze back on God instead of focusing so much on the details of the journey I wanted Him to be orchestrating. Their words were convicting. I think that oftentimes we would argue that we are open to God authoring our stories when, in actuality, we are trying in our own strength to conveniently squeeze God into the story we've prewritten ourselves. It's important to keep things in perspective. To let God be God and understand that what's asked of us is just to follow faithfully. When we cut our gaze off of our own creations and set our eyes on the Creator of all things, we are able to approach life with greater clarity.

> All a person's ways seem pure to them,
>    but motives are weighed by the LORD.
> Commit to the LORD whatever you do,
>    and he will establish your plans. . . .
> In their hearts humans plan their course,
>    but the LORD establishes their steps. (Prov. 16:2–3, 9)

I spent time chewing on this Scripture for a while. It was as mysterious as it was intimidating, because it didn't offer me any direct answers. But it was comforting knowing that it didn't read, "Commit to the Lord whatever you do, and then good luck figuring the rest out." I found that the longer I spent time with these words, the more they offered me a rest-filled peace. I knew God had given me specific talents and skills and strengths, and I could trust that even when I didn't have all the answers, He was charting a course for me.

## Saying Yes to God

It took me a while to see the clearest sign God was laying directly in front of me. As days passed and I struggled to discover what the Lord would have for me, speaking requests continued to flood in and I found myself flying back and forth all around the country. When the light bulb finally went on in my mind that perhaps He intended me to be a professional speaker, I couldn't believe that there could be a way I could make a living out of something I loved so much. Especially not at age twenty-three and without any clue how to run a ministry. But the requests kept coming in, and as ill-equipped as I felt to be about such holy business, I started to simply say yes to all of the big and small things.

There's truth in the popular expression, "God doesn't call the equipped, He equips the called." As believers, we are instructed to put His creation to work—to exercise the hands and feet and brain He gave us to be about His business and contribute to society. But throughout each season we are also encouraged to hold our plans loosely. To always be willing to surrender our own personal direction to follow the direction God leads—even when we feel helpless or ill-prepared to carry out the new journey. It's that type of focused work ethic and desperate dependence that enables Him to equip us fully and mold us into the tools He needs us to be. I've found that the times we feel least capable of something are the same times He reveals Himself most mightily.

I quickly realized that I had gone from uncomfortable to uncommon. Not many other people my age were doing what I was doing. I didn't have any resources to turn to for guidance or specific direction. But my lack of familiarity was what forced a raw and abiding faith and dependency on God. Day by day I was forced to trust that God would provide new opportunities. Week by week I was forced to trust that He would provide a way for me and sustain consistency. Month by month I was forced to trust that He would make ends meet, financially. With every day and week and month that passed where true trust was forced from me, I found that my faith grew and the weight of expectation I carried on my own abilities lightened. I started to understand what it actually meant to boldly trust in the Lord with all my heart and lean not on my own understanding; to submit to Him in all my ways as He made my path straight (see Prov. 3:5–6). When I finally had the courage to surrender my own life plans, He revealed to me so much more abundance in the work of His own hands.

With every bold and courageous yes, I found my life adventure growing. A faith based around saying yes to God opened the most amazing doors. In the course of just a year or two it lead me to so many incredible places. I found my way to the summit of Mt. Kilimanjaro, sharing the gospel and washing the feet of weary porters along the way. To the slums of Uganda, holding and loving on children and adults dealing with disease, whom society had turned its back to. To the streets of Costa Rica, praying over young prostitutes and helping move mountains with growing ministries needing farming space. And to the prisons of Baton Rouge, encouraging and speaking life to incarcerated dads reunited with their children for a day. All in Jesus Christ's name.

I found myself speaking all across the nation—sharing my testimony, unpacking the gospel, and proclaiming the Good News. As incredible as the highs were, the yeses also lead me to the smallest places. And when my pride began to creep in and my ego started to trip me up and convince me those smaller venues were less significant, the Spirit spoke truth through a friend who helped me reframe my perspective again.

### Embracing Your Mission Field

> Whatever you do, work at it with all your heart, as working for the Lord, not for human masters, since you know that you will receive an inheritance from the Lord as a reward. It is the Lord Christ you are serving. (Col. 3:23–24)

Too often we allow the enemy to convince us we are in a job or a circumstance or a family or a school where we are ineffective to be used as God's own tool. We feel like we're stuck or we're wasting our time or we're in an environment where we can't really use our gifts and talents for God. But the fact of the matter is that this perspective is a lie we have to actively combat and eventually break through. God is a King of purposeful sovereignty, and He is always in the business of using you.

It takes creativity, at times, to see life through a King-view and embrace how He is possibly using us in the places we are. It's easy to covet the position others are in. To become jealous of how someone else is being used. But, in truth, God has a perfect purpose for the day, the hour, and the specific place He has you. He desires to use your specific skills and talents and strengths in the exact setting you're in, for whatever season of time He intends. It's trusting in that truth that broadens our narrow perspectives and allows our attention to shift to the mission field He's already led us to.

Would you consider yourself a missionary? It's a title that, for a long time, I only saw through a thin and tilted view. I thought missionaries were only those believers off in foreign countries, evangelizing in the slums or remote bush villages of unreached nations or planting churches across the world and relying solely on support-raising. I thought the role of a missionary was exclusive and unobtainable. A coveted calling that God put on the hearts of only the boldest believers—the ones willing to radically give everything up in order to follow Him.

But then one day someone asked me what I did for a living. I always cringed at that question because my answer was never as clean and packaged as a nine-to-five job. I always fumbled for words and awkwardly tried to explain that I traveled place to place sharing my story, and that I blogged and wrote in faith that God would use my broken words to impact somebody. I didn't know how to explain that I just blindly trusted, each day, that God was using me, but before I could finish my tangled words this time, he said, "Oh, you're a missionary." I stared at him for a moment and clarified that none of the places I was traveling were exotic or unreached. Primarily they were mundane—churches, community gatherings, events, and various retreats.

"Right, so you're a missionary," he repeated. "I'm a missionary too. I teach at my town's public high school and help coach a football team for the youth."

I must have looked ridiculously confused, because he went on to explain to me that since we were both believers we were inevitably focused on loving others well, being about God's business, and sharing His truth. That we may be in more "average" places, but that that type of Kingdom work was exactly what missionaries did. He challenged me to see every place I spent time in as a new mission field. He reminded me that, in Christ, I looked different. That wherever I was and whatever I was doing, people were watching me. If I lived my life understanding that I was a missionary, would I not live with more awareness and more intention? "Whatever you do in word or deed, do all in the name of the Lord Jesus, giving thanks through Him to God the Father" (Col. 3:17 NASB).

I heard an awesome quote one time that simply said, "Wherever you are, be all there." I think it's important we understand that God knows exactly how He is using us and what plans He has for our lives. It is up to us to embrace the purpose He has for us, work diligently to be about His business, hold our plans loosely, be ready to surrender ourselves to Christ, and say yes to God when He prompts us to move—fully trusting that His plans are holy and good.

# 12

## The Bold Life

As far as I felt I had come, God still had a lot of heart-work to do in me. When it came to loving others as boldly as Christ loved me, I had a lot to learn. And to be honest, I still do. So much of my spiritual journey revolved around myself. My brokenness, my lack of understanding, my revelation, my healing, my new journey. But while the gospel encounters us personally in order to set us free, it never stops with us. Ever. It always grows to reach other people's needs. That is what marks the difference between a journey from broken to beautiful and a journey from broken to bold—the fact that for whatever reason God chooses to include us in the continued story. He chooses to use us, boldly, to breathe out the same life that was first breathed into us.

The Great Commission makes that clear in Matthew 28:18–20.

Then Jesus came to [the disciples] and said, "All authority in heaven and on earth has been given to me. Therefore go and make disciples of all nations, baptizing them in the name of the Father and of the Son and of the Holy Spirit, and teaching them to obey everything I have commanded you. And surely I am with you always, to the very end of the age."

Trying to figure out all the ways I could be reaching others more intentionally was intimidating. I yearned for my newfound boldness to also include boldness in sharing Christ more personally with other people. I began to understand that it wasn't too hard to *act* like Christ. What was challenging was to *react* like Christ, particularly in the moments when life was challenging and more was required of me. The nature of our hearts shine through in these moments of response and reaction, and it was in those times others would be able to see Christ in me most clearly. So rather than praying God would just download truth into me, I began praying for opportunity. I found that the situations He placed me in and the circumstances He began to bring me through almost always fit into one or more of three callings: to love deeply, to forgive freely, and to march boldly with a holy army.

## Love Deeply

A new command I give you: Love one another. As I have loved you, so you must love one another. By this everyone will know you are my disciples, if you love one another. (John 13:34–35)

A spiritual mentor of mine once taught me that a woman should never pursue a man. A woman should pursue a deeper, more intimate relationship with Christ, and, in turn, the man God would eventually inspire to pursue *her* would be drawn nearer to Him as he peeled back the layers of who she was, in Christ.

164

When it came to Jeremiah Lee Aiken, I semi-listened to that advice. My "Kissless Till Next Christmas," year-long intimacy fast was rapidly approaching its second birthday, and I had loved my season of singleness in Christ. But when I was first introduced to Jeremiah, I could have stared at him all night. In fact, I think I did. He was the most attractive man I'd ever seen. His presence was captivating. It didn't hurt that he loved Jesus fiercely. And that he had an air of gentleness and humility about him that was intoxicating. I won't go so far as to say that I threw myself at him, but when he first asked for my number it took me about four seconds to decide that I loved Jesus and Jesus loved me, but I was ready to be dating. *Immediately.*

After nine months of dating, I knew in my heart that Jeremiah was the man I longed to marry. After fifteen months of dating, I was prepared, at any moment, for him to take a knee. In fact, I was egging it on. Let's be honest: I had already picked out the ring. I expected the proposal to come, but I never would have expected that once Jeremiah did take that knee, God would begin teaching me some of the greatest lessons about what it truly meant, biblically, to love another deeply.

My whole life I'd been sold "happily ever after," time and time again. In the movies. On TV. On Facebook, Pinterest, YouTube, you name it. I'd heard talk about "Prince Charming," "the One," my "soul mate." Even in church, I'd been told that God was designing the *perfect* man for me. That there was *one* out there who would complete me. While I'd always rolled my eyes at those concepts, particularly after all I'd learned through my spiritual fasting, I had still failed to realize how much they had subtly etched their way into my thoughts and heart.

I'd loved seeing my relationship with Jeremiah unfold. We'd navigated the highs and lows of dating. We'd stumbled and struggled. We'd shared great victories and highs. We'd cried some, laughed often, bickered more, and smiled the most. We'd supported one another in the struggles of building our careers. We'd seen financial blessings and we'd been broke-as-a-joke. We'd been faithfully committed to one another and held one another accountable to purity. We'd wrestled conviction and repented openly to one another. We'd praised and worshiped together, we'd struggled and sinned together, we'd crawled back to the foot of the cross together. We'd fallen in love with one another's families, we'd wasted days away dreaming of our own future family. We'd worked out together, vegged out together, and rocked out together. We'd worked through book studies with one another, traveled with one another, been beyond annoyed with one another. We'd comforted one another, danced with one another, and respected one another. We'd navigated through the year and ultimately, every day, chosen to grow in love with each other.

Yet when Jeremiah asked me to be his wife on one chilly February night, I immediately doubted my answer.

I knew I couldn't have been the only girl in the world who cried tears of joy with a new ring on her finger while wrestling the overwhelming weight of the yes that just escaped her lips. I knew I couldn't have been the only girl whose mind had begun spinning when the hypothetical dreams became the reality of the moment. I knew I couldn't have been the only girl who wondered why her "fairytale" moment wasn't as ridiculously blissful and simple as the four hundred thousand movies had made it seem. I knew I couldn't have been the only girl who had ever felt guilty for even harboring that range of emotion. But the fact of the matter was that as soon as the boyfriend I cherished became the fiancé I promise to cherish for the *rest of my life*, my human nature began to doubt. And I began to realize how much, in regard to love, my mind and heart had been crafted by the world rather than the Word.

You see, the world says there is a soul mate. The world says there is a Prince Charming. The world says there is a *perfect person* for you out there, and if you find them you will live happily ever after. If you do marry the wrong one, it's not the end of the world; you can just divorce them and continue the hunt for the one made *just* for you. The one who will always make you happy. But if you want the least amount of hassle possible, make sure you find the perfect one the first time around.

The world says the person should be perfect for *you*. The ring should be perfect for *you*. The proposal should be perfect for *you*. The wedding should be perfect for *you*. And the Pinterest world will certainly praise *you*. If you manage to host the perfect barn wedding, that is.

But the Word says it has nothing to do with you. The Word says the covenant of marriage has everything to do with God. The Word says the journey of navigating a lifetime promise of abiding love has everything to do with Jesus. And the only thing perfect for *you* in the equation is grace.

My mind doubted because I was weighed down with the fear of making the wrong choice. Maybe Jeremiah wasn't "the One." How would I know for sure? There were things we disagreed on. There were things about him that didn't always make me happy. It had been a challenge, at times, to love him. I knew it had also been a challenge, at times, for him to love me. Maybe we were just compatible and I was making the wrong decision. How would I know, for sure, that he was my soul mate?

But in my doubt and my prayer and my questioning, I quickly realized that maybe, just maybe, I had it all backwards. God revealed to me that marriage was a covenant—a promise—to God that we would vow to love another like Christ first loved us. In the most intimate, challenging, all-inclusive way. With a deep, abiding love that mirrored His unfailing grace. It was a vow to become one flesh with another person. To serve them and selflessly love them as Christ served and selflessly loved us to the cross. To carry their burdens. To take the lashes of their shortcomings. To bear the taunting of their sins and struggles. I was to put Jeremiah before myself, to the point of brokenness, so that we could ultimately rise, just as our King did, in love. With a greater understanding of the magnitude of the gospel. With a greater appreciation for the power of what Jesus did on our behalf.

God revealed to me that marriage was a taste—a tiny, intimate taste of His love for us. A promise that was not measured lightly because, ultimately, it was a promise to accept another and love another like God loved us. It was nothing I could even come close to doing on my own. And *that* became the joy of saying yes to the proposal. Not that I had found my "perfect" person, but that he and I were a step closer to drawing back a layer and getting to see God's perfect love played out in a beautiful way in our lives.

I became excited about marrying Jeremiah because he was not the perfect man for me. And I was not the perfect woman for him. But we were both committed to following the perfect King who showed us the perfect example of how to truly love, deeply.

I was overwhelmed that God would allow me—messy, baggage-carrying, selfish, emotional me—to have the honor and privilege of loving and caring for His sweet child Jeremiah. I knew the minute I believed I was capable of selflessly and unconditionally loving him, I would fail. But it brought the sweetest joy to my heart to know that I didn't have to go at it alone. God was with me. God was with us. Through Him, all things were possible. Including a deep love that mirrored the love God had for me.

I began to learn that the ultimate wreckage of self was available to me through the covenant of marriage, and that the greatest challenge I would ever journey through would keep me in a state of voluntary wreckage for years to come. But that hard love, that tough and holy love, would grant me a partner to walk through life-lived discipleship with and would shape me into more of the image of Christ than everything else.

I also realized that deep love God revealed to me was applicable to so many other relationships. To every other person around me. That loving others deeply was hard, and messy, and inconvenient at times, but it was the clearest picture of God's grace. That every single person I came into contact with was going to spend eternity in one of two places, and I needed to love like that was a *big deal*. By loving others deeply I was truthfully preaching the gospel—even more so than when I used words. And that deep and present and sacrificial love was the same love that would require everything of me but would ultimately set my heart free.

### Forgive Freely

In order to love Jeremiah fully, and to love others fully, I knew I had a lingering piece of bondage that still needed to be broken through. I couldn't live boldly and I couldn't love deeply if the bondage of unforgiveness still owned me. If I wanted my life to boldly echo Christ's life, then unforgiveness couldn't hold a place in my story. It was the antithesis of the cross—after all, who are we to withhold forgiveness from one another when God has never withheld forgiveness from us?

Loving others deeply doesn't just apply to those whom we have peace with and whom it feels good to love. Living boldly and loving deeply looks like forgiving freely, no matter whom that forgiveness must be outstretched toward.

That's a hard concept to wrap our heads around. Because, in truth, there is probably someone sitting on the forefront of your mind whom you have been so wronged by that the thought of forgiveness is nauseating. Maybe it was the abuse. Or the rape. Or the theft. Or the deceit. We can think of ten thousand reasons why the people we don't want to forgive don't deserve forgiveness for all they put us through. But the fact of the matter is the longer you withhold forgiveness from another, the longer they own a piece of you. And if we believe Christ has bought us, in full, at the price of His own life, then we are robbing ourselves of the freedom that grace grants us when we allow another person to mentally or emotionally or spiritually hold possession over that piece of us.

Maybe it was the infidelity. Or the gossip. Or the abandonment. Maybe it was the suicide. That was the dark chain that still wrapped itself around me.

I had healed in so many ways. It had been years since my dad's death. But I still harbored resentment toward a man I still believed, at the core, was a coward. A man who had run from the mess he made and taken a foolish way out. A man who had left a wife and two daughters to put back the pieces of a shattered life. Deep down, I blamed so much of my wandering and my promiscuity and my struggles on my dad. Sometimes that was the easier way to process things—to dismiss them as cause-and-effect results of another person's shortcomings.

But, in truth, my resentment and my anger and my frustrations were really just rationalizations for a heart that was calloused from years of unforgiveness. My soul still reeked of blame. And while I understood how all-inclusively Christ had forgiven me, I just couldn't surrender the cemented belief, deep down, that my dad's actions weren't forgivable.

But in Ephesians 4:31–32, there was a word that stood out to me and helped peel back an unexpected layer in the process of forgiving freely. "Get rid of all bitterness, rage and anger, brawling and slander, along with every form of malice. Be kind and *compassionate* to one another, forgiving each other, just as in Christ God forgave you" (emphasis added).

Compassion. Sympathy and concern for the misfortunes of others. After I came across those words, compassion was a seed God planted in me and began to nourish. A new thought began to slowly reframe my perspective of forgiveness. My prayers shifted from, "God, help me forgive more freely," to "God, you have known the greatest compassion for me in my failings. I long to look more like you. Will you nurture a heart of compassion within me?"

I saw him first as a little boy. My daddy. With his soft olive skin and his round face. Carefree and joy-filled and innocent. A simple Southern boy with two parents who loved him deeply.

I saw him as a young teen, bouncing around from school to school with each of his dad's job transfers. Moving from football team to football team, trying to establish his footing. Maybe he was bullied—or struggled to feel like he ever really fit any one place. Uprooted every time he'd finally made a name for himself among his teammates.

I saw him as a college football player and, eventually, a law student. Navigating the dating scene and balancing his course load. I smiled to imagine what he must have been like so near to me in age—and laughed remembering the time he told me he once dated a girl with the nickname "Toot." I wondered what his friends had been like, and what had stirred his passion for law.

I saw him as a young man meeting and falling for my beautiful mom. I imagined the butterflies he must have felt as he watched her glide down the aisle. The excitement and nervousness he must have known as he took on the role of husband and they dreamed of their future family.

I could almost feel the warm tears that rolled down his cheeks as he helped deliver my sister and me. As he navigated the highs and lows of carrying the title of Daddy. As he wrestled with the pressures of raising preteen girls and the expectation of providing for a busy family.

I ached for how his heart must have broken with the death of his own daddy. How deeply he must have grieved. And I smiled thinking about the laughter he brought to the basketball court as he volunteered his time to coach Special Olympians and other athletes with disabilities.

I ached for the stress and pressure he must have felt when work was tough and money was tight and everything in him wanted to seem strong for his family. And I saw him in a new light as I thought about the demons he admitted to wrestling. The strangleholds that gripped him sexually, in regards to his struggles with pornography. The pride that must have felt so damaged by Satan's relentless taunts and schemes.

I thought about his insecurities. His deep-rooted weaknesses. And how similar he and I truly were in so many broken ways. I saw the man who was always able to love others far more than he was ever able to love himself sitting on the edge of that hotel bed, his heart pounding and his hands trembling.

My heart broke for that innocent Southern boy who had truly believed life wasn't worth it and gave up. The olive-skinned baby who had seen a lot of life and who was worn out and tired and aching.

Compassion bred forgiveness because it allowed me to see another human as just that—human. Worn and ravaged and navigating a broken world, just like me. It gave a history to the action that had wronged me and opened up a broader perspective to understand that even people who have wronged us so deeply have a story—a reason why sin has a stronghold in their lives. Hurt people hurt people. I wasn't instructed to withhold forgiveness from the hurting; I was instructed to be kind and compassionate, having mercy on the lost and wandering, just as God had mercy on me.

Grace had been extended to me. And I was being called to grace. By finally forgiving my father, I encountered an intimacy with Christ that stretched away from logic and made sense of the nonsensical and introduced me to a different kind of humility. A Jesus-kind of humility that had everything to do with God and little to do with me. I had been foolish to mistake kindness for weakness—the strength of a lion can exist within the spirit of a lamb. Forgiveness is selfless strength. If we want to look even a bit like Jesus, we must embrace the willingness to forgive freely.

## The Holy Army

It would be foolish to believe that when we make Jesus Christ the Lord of our lives Satan steps back, counts his losses, and moves on. That's far from the truth. The enemy is bitter. Resentful. Keen. Individuals in pursuit of a closer relationship with Christ are often targeted, tested, and tempted. A life lived in faith doesn't exempt us from hardship or wreckage or suffering, but there is a difference in how those in Christ combat Satan's schemes. When the Holy Spirit dwells within our hearts, we enter battle in the midst of a holy army. We face temptation with the strength of a King on our side and the love of a gentle Father who picks us up when we fall. We enter valleys with a divine hope carrying us through, and we're equipped with an armor of God that wields righteousness, readiness, faith, salvation, and the Spirit of His unending truth (Eph. 6:10–18).

I find that one of the greatest assets to living boldly is the unbelievable blessing found in accountability and community. Battle becomes infinitely easier when the holy army that can rise up alongside us is a holy army we also do life with, daily. Proverbs 13:20 reads, "Walk with the wise and become wise, for a companion of fools suffers harm." Loving deeply and forgiving freely comes to life when we have brothers and sisters in Christ marching forward with us, arm-in-arm. Through community and accountability God desires for us to trust in Him and surrender our lives to Him to the ultimate point of giving up our lives for one another, just as Christ did. In prayer, in fellowship, in confession, and in trust, we are invited to live life as a body of believers, led by bold love.

I love my community—my holy army. It's something I lacked so deeply for so many years—and now is one of my greatest blessings. One of my sisters in Christ, in particular, has taught me so much about what it means to do life with someone authentically. Even when life is hard. And raw. And frustrating.

Molly and I met under the messiest of circumstances during my senior year. She was a brand-new transfer onto LSU's soccer team and a brand-new believer to boot. Our mutual sense of humor that no one else seemed to find funny meant immediate and over-the-top bonding—complete with razor scooter rides around our apartment complex and late-night sessions learning "Hot Cross Buns" on the recorder and costumed runs to get frozen yogurt in town. We were weird.

We were also two sinners saved by grace with messy pasts and a lot of repercussions for our sins still echoing through our lives. Mine were easier to conceal and deal with privately. But hers were on display for the world to see. None more clearly than the positive pregnancy test that interrupted everything.

I watched as a repercussion of Molly's previous sexual sin literally came to life within her. I felt beyond helpless as we cried together that hot August afternoon, and I journeyed with her as she weighed the costs of all she would be losing. Then I stood back, and stood in awe, as I watched Molly, a brand-new believer, stand up against a lot of opposing opinion and choose Christ, who unwaveringly chose life for her sweet baby.

On a day when it seemed like the world was ending, we cried hard. But I began learning from her, seeing what it looked like to be soaked in mercy and grace, and we couldn't help but feel like God was purposing a special story. Binding together a friendship that was different—and heart-wrecking—and important.

We lost touch for a bit after she withdrew from LSU and moved back home to Arizona to complete her pregnancy, but God never stopped pressing her on my heart. And in praying through what *community* really meant in His eyes, and what sharing life with someone looked like even when it was

175

challenging, we reconnected and found our stride walking as sisters in Christ.

Four years later we haven't missed a beat. We've done life together every single day with half of the country between us. I've had the privilege of watching Molly raise her incredibly beautiful daughter, and I've studied her every move, knowing that when I welcome a child of my own, I will want to follow her example. Our friendship has taken us to the mission field in Africa and to the rainforests of Costa Rica, where she wept in joy beside me as I said "I do." It has held tight through break-ups, way-too-late-night phone calls, lots of tears, lots of sin, and lots of grace. It has waded through the loss of her sweet brother, the completion of her college degree, and the amazing journey she is now on, rocking it with the Arizona FCA team.

She keeps my stomach hurting from laughing so hard, my head hurting from how frustrating she can be, and my heart yearning for more of God as I see Him pour out of her, daily. She is as equally ridiculous as she is insightful—the kind of insightful that makes the holy Word crawl off of the page and mean something, every single day. We're so deeply different. And some days that's intensely frustrating. But every day it's overwhelmingly rewarding to know I have a sister like Molly woven into my story.

Because when all is said and done, and adversity has inevitably punctured our lives and brokenness has found its way into our story and we've come to know pain and suffering, community helps remind us of the promises of God that guarantee He has overcome the world and that there is more. From the ashes and the broken pieces, let us not forget that "these three [things] remain: faith, hope and love. But the greatest of these is love" (1 Cor. 13:13), and we are fiercely loved by a sovereign

King who empowers us to fiercely love our sisters and brothers, in spite of everything. We are able to invite others to step out of their wreckage and step into a journey where they can voluntarily allow God to wreck their lives for His glory.

As a result, we'll become a generation that stands forever faithful to the One who makes broken things bold. The One who wrecks our lives to save our lives, and invites us into His story. We'll stand firm in His promises, even when they're challenging. We'll forever appreciate the truth in the holy Scripture that mightily breathes,

> My suffering was good for me,
>> for it taught me to pay attention to your decrees.
> (Ps. 119:71 NLT)

# Conclusion

Writing this book was more of a battle than I expected it to be. I've found that the enemy tends to attack us most fiercely in the midst of kingdom work, in the wake of pure efforts that could prove to be faith-strengthening and community-building and God-glorifying. I've also found that it's easy, even as a believer who has been walking hand-in-hand with Christ for years, to doubt my effectiveness or question whether I'm even worthy of being used by God. To be disheartened by the internal voice that raises every kind of doubt and makes me overthink the simple and complicate the clear-cut and forget that God is doing a good work through me, not due to me.

It can be infinitely intimidating to share our own stories. To air out our baggage and confess our sins publicly and find the right words to make sense of the messy. I think it's one of the hardest things, really—to share our testimonies. But then again, why wouldn't it be? Scripture itself declares that Satan is defeated by the blood of the Lamb and by the word of our testimonies (see Rev. 12:11). If our boldness and our willingness to give voice to our vulnerability has the power to completely obliterate the enemy, should we expect him to go down easily? No. Satan puts up a fight—often an internal battle—that tries to convince us there is no power in our stories.

But what I love about a living, breathing relationship with God is that it centers around our brokenness and it makes a home amid our vulnerability. There is inherent humility in the gospel of Jesus Christ. To say that we've been set free is to confess we were bound up. To say that we've been washed clean is to confess we were impure. To say that we've been made new is to confess we were full of broken things. The beauty in all of those confessions is that they echo with glory.

You are not alone. Romans 3:23 reminds us that "all have sinned and fall short of the glory of God." First Corinthians 10:13 assures us that "no temptation has overtaken [us] except what is common to mankind." My prayer is that you find rest in the truth that every one of us has baggage and every one of us carries a story. But you are promised that if you "humble yourselves before the Lord . . . he *will* lift you up" (James 4:10, emphasis added). So I also pray you begin to let God breathe boldness into your lungs and that the words of your testimony flow out freely. Because you are valuable, and you are loved, and God is orchestrating, through you, a powerful kingdom story.

The enemy would love for us to stay silent—to keep our sin in the shadows and feel like we are alone in our suffering. I hope, if this book has served any purpose at all, it has empowered you to realize connection and community are built through our transparency. There is no shame in bold authenticity. Your brokenness has the power to be transformed into boldness by the King who is authoring your story.

# Acknowledgments

To Jeremiah, my one and only—thank you for choosing me. For humbly leading me. For relentlessly loving me. Thank you for putting up with my constant craziness and for taking big and bold and blind leaps of faith with me. Thank you for challenging me, for comforting me, and for never being shy to call me out for all the clever ways I tried to disguise my procrastination. You are my greatest adventure and the clearest picture of Christ's love I've ever seen. Writing this book during our first year of marriage was hard. Moving through pregnancy at the same time was harder. But honoring you by becoming a Tampa Bay Buccaneers fan was the hardest challenge of all. So I hope it's clear to you, now, that I love you unconditionally.

To Bill and Teresa—thank you for clicking the link to that random blog post and for taking the time to read my rambling words. Thank you for believing in the potential and tracking me down and breathing unexpected hope and excitement into my lifelong dream. The countless phone calls, the unfailing encouragement, the patience and the coaching—thank you for every step from start to finish of making this dream a reality. But most of all, thank you for your friendship and your authentic dedication to God's calling in your lives. You two are a killer tag-team!

To Rebekah Guzman and the Baker team—thank you all for believing in me so deeply and for pursuing this clueless, first-time author so passionately. Your commitment to this project has taught me so much about the power of community. I've been blessed by the opportunity to learn all about this wild world of publishing with you all by my side and I can't wait to see what the future holds as we move forward as a team.

Last but not least, to my sweet mommy—you are truly a prize, and I love you so deeply. Thank you for twenty-six years of relentlessly praying for me. Thank you for trusting God, even when it was beyond challenging, and for always honoring my privacy and freedom to navigate my own journey. Thank you for letting me share our lives so candidly and for trusting me to steward some of the hardest parts of our family's story. Thank you for the countless hours of listening to me read what I had written, for your honest and blunt feedback, and for always laughing at me even when I'm not that funny. Thank you for all you have taught me about being a godly wife, a loving mother, and a brave daughter of the Most High King. I will always be your baby, and I'm so grateful God chose you to be my mom.

# About the Author

I wish this section of the book read "About the Reader," because I'm pretty tired of talking about myself and I'm anxious to know more about who took the time to hunker down and dig into this book to explore its rambling pages. Thank you for piecing through my story. For coming back to each chapter and walking with me through my journey and sitting with me through the lessons I learned along the way. I wish we could be curled up on my couch, instead, talking life and Jesus and *your* story. Maybe one day! It's an open-door policy here at the Aiken home, so if you're passing through Atlanta, let us know.

There's something about the author you might not have known—I'm actually now an Aiken. Mary Morlan Aiken. But I still go by my maiden name for the sake of street cred. And because Mo Isom is almost spelled the same forward and backward.

I married my best friend, Jeremiah Aiken, in September 2014, and we welcomed our beautiful daughter, Auden, in December

2015. We live in Georgia with our two dog-ters, Jacey and Penny (think moderately priced department store), and when I'm not writing, blogging, or traveling to speak, you can usually find us sprawled out in our pajamas watching football, exploring the best places to eat around the city, or spending time with our friends and family. We love our home church, Passion City, and are so grateful to be part of a church community that is always exploring new and radical ways to serve Jesus, worship boldly, and grow as a family.

I feel like my story is still being written, as I'm sure yours is too. I would love to hear from you, get to know you, and hear how this book challenged or encouraged you. You can connect with me through any of the outlets below. And if you're really weird and still haven't had enough, you can jump over to my blog to read more of my writing. Can't wait to connect with you!

www.MoIsom.com
Twitter: www.twitter.com/MoIsom
Instagram: www.instagram.com/MoIsom
Facebook: www.facebook.com/TheMoIsom

## JOURNEYING FROM BROKEN TO BOLD

### CONNECT WITH

# Mo Isom

🐦 @MoIsom

f Facebook.com/TheMoIsom

📷 @MoIsom

▶ Momonstr

If you're interested in booking Mo
to speak at your next event or would like to
check her availability and fee schedule,

## VISIT MOISOM.COM

# LIKE THIS
# BOOK?
## Consider sharing it with others!

- Share or mention the book on your social media platforms. Use the hashtag **#WreckMyLife**.

- Write a book review on your blog or on a retailer site.

- Pick up a copy for friends, family, or strangers! Anyone who you think would enjoy and be challenged by its message.

- Share this message on Twitter or Facebook: **"I loved #WreckMyLife by @MoIsom //MoIsom.com @ReadBakerBooks."**

- Recommend this book for your church, workplace, book club, or class.

- Follow Baker Books on social media and tell us what you like.

 Facebook.com/ReadBakerBooks

 @ReadBakerBooks